Peaceable
School

Vicky Schreiber Dill

Cover design by
Victoria Voelker

Cover illustration by
Christopher Ganz

Phi Delta Kappa Educational Foundation
408 North Union Street
Post Office Box 789
Bloomington, Indiana 47402-0789
U.S.A.

Printed in the United States of America

Library of Congress Catalog Card Number 98-68217
ISBN 0-87367-810-9

Dedication

To friends in the work of peace:
Delia, Jo, Marty, Martin, Wok

and to
My mother and my family,
especially the children,
Emily, Isaac, and Moses,
who say they think this book
will make a big difference.

Table of Contents

Introduction

On 12 December 1995 in San Antonio, local news reported the murder of a 12-year-old boy. He was murdered because he was trying to get out of a gang. Just the day before, this same youth and undoubtedly the friend who shot him and several other gang members were attending Taft High School.

Children are murdered when they stay in the gangs, and they are murdered when they try to get out. How can the American public understand this tragic dilemma? How can parents send their children to schools where gangs and other youths are capable of such violence? How can children live with the fear of seeing their fathers and mothers going into such schools to teach, their brothers and sisters to learn?

To comprehend school violence, one must understand more than just the violence that occurs in schools. The classroom reflects the violence in the community and nation.

Both classroom violence and the larger phenomenon might be understood in terms of one image: that of many walls. Our nation is frantically building walls to keep out dangerous people. These walls surround more than just gated communities and moneyed estates, more than just middle-class apartment complexes and housing developments. Increasingly, towns are surrounding themselves with walls. Politicians have proposed building a triple-fence barrier across our entire southern border. And there are more abstract — though just as secure — walls built with spray cans, gang colors, and guns.

Walls are a direct response to fear, but this frenetic fortification provides no real sense of security. Fear spreads over walls. And it is this real and keenly perceived sense of vulnerability that underlies every discussion of violence.

Concerns about safety are especially pressing for the 12 million poor children and their teachers who go to school in urban centers, such as New York, Baltimore, Houston, and Los Angeles. Teachers and students in these areas usually have no choice about the schools they attend. These parents believe, and are generally correct, that their children are at greater risk than those in suburban or rural areas (Gutscher 1993, p. 10). But the fear of school violence is no longer just an urban or poverty issue. Danger in public schools pervades all geographic locations and types of neighborhood (Duhon-Haynes, Albert, and Duhon-Ross 1995, pp. 7-10).

Into this national fear walk the public school children with their naive hope for education. They come to day care, Head Start, and kindergarten. For far too many, their encounter with school is their only chance for a better future.

But what if those hopeful children are met with bullies and even bullets? And what if no one can change that? What if, instead of teaching, the teachers merely patrol their classes? What if all the child will learn is what negative behavior elicits which punishment?

In the last two decades, the nation's intense fears have led to rote recitation of the "zero tolerance" mantra. Ask any principal about violence in his or her school and the first response will be, "We have zero tolerance for violence." In many cases, the words, "zero tolerance," mean that educators have developed a siege mentality. Students must carry transparent backpacks, but they do not learn conflict resolution. They learn to walk in straight rows between classes, but they do not experience full-fledged anti-violence campaigns. The increasingly popular administrative posture of inflexibility, toughness, and swift, harsh punishment gives the public only a superficial reassurance that the school is "safe" (Noguera 1996, p. 190).

Indeed, the new "safe" schools look no different from very dangerous ones. They are surrounded by high fences. Metal signs are bolted to the front of the building, warning, "No Guns, No

2

Smoking, No Drinking, No Drugs." There are lists of what the school does not allow, but there is no indication of what the school nurtures.

All who work, move, and live in and around schools need sound, easily accessible, commonsense research to guide their thinking about issues of school safety and violence prevention. This book is designed to provide not only a framework for thinking about violence, but some specific solutions as well. It provides the general principles and guidelines of school safety for educators, parents, and anyone involved in schools.

This book makes no effort to tout any single solution or program. Any effort to reduce violence must address each element of an individual school's problems; and thus individual programs will vary widely. However, what all effective solutions have in common is the power to move both aggressors and victims beyond their visible or psychological walls toward coexistence on mutual turf, whether it be city streets, malls, parks, or the schoolyard.

The book begins with an in-depth look at a question currently being debated nationwide: Is the problem of school violence real? Some sources suggest minimum levels of escalation; others prophesy with doomsday data. Do perceptions match reality? Are weapons proliferating in the schools, or do we just hear about them more frequently? Do the media report incidents of school violence consistently? Are urban students really more at risk? Is there safety in the country? Chapter One also looks at the role of denial in the problem of school violence. Why do some organizations and individuals want to hide the problem? What happens if this denial continues?

Chapter Two explores how some schools manage to make matters worse by the ways in which they deal with students. It provides guidelines for educators to make their schools more safe and humane places.

Chapter Three explores the culture of violence and suggests ways to turn that to a culture of nonviolence. The chapter presents eight principles that educators must understand if they are to create less violent schools.

Chapter Four focuses on the actions and responsibilities of administrators who want to turn their school around. In addition to specific actions the administrator should take, the chapter also discusses the leadership characteristics that are necessary for an administrator to succeed in creating a nonviolent school.

Chapter Five focuses on teacher behaviors and attitudes that reduce violence. The chapter provides specific guidelines for teachers of elementary, middle, and high schools.

Chapter Six examines some of the resources that are available to support schools that want to change their culture. These support services come not only from law enforcement agencies and health departments but from a variety of sources that educators sometimes overlook.

Readers who wish to know about specific violence prevention programs are encouraged to contact the organizations listed in the Selected Resources section. Many of these organizations are willing to work closely with schools to design a plan to decrease violence and build resilience in youth.

The nature of the school's response to violence is no small matter. It is a matter of life and death for most youth.

References

Duhon-Haynes, Gwendolyn M.; Albert, Harry.; and Duhon-Ross, Alice. "Variations in Violence." In *Dealing with Youth Violence: What Schools and Communities Need to Know*, edited by Rose M. Duhon-Sells. Bloomington, Ind.: National Educational Service, 1995.

Gutscher, Cecile. "Violence in Schools: Death Threat for Reform?" *America's Agenda* 3 (Fall 1993): 10.

Hull, Jon D. "The State of the Union." *Time*, 30 January 1995, p. 63.

Noguera, Pedro A. "The Critical State of Violence Prevention." *School Administrator* 53 (February 1996).

Chapter One

How Violence Comes to School

The school's front door is no barrier to violence in the community. This was well understood by rural Washington superintendent David Rawles, who noted, "All the bars, metal detectors, and security guards in the world can't protect us." He spoke these words shortly after a 14-year-old student, armed with a hunting rifle, allegedly shot and killed a teacher and two students and critically wounded another student ("School Shooting," 1996).

National, regional, local, and neighborhood crime trends all influence the nature of the challenges and opportunities that educators face. School leaders should understand that these trends often are reflected in the schools in ways that teachers may not recognize. The violence in students' environments or families often is expressed in their behaviors and attitudes. Societal violence may explain why one student postures for the teacher while another of a similar background is willing to learn and risk; why one student is scared to walk into the bathroom and so is miserable all day, while still another simply drops out.

Fortunately, the national crime rate has been decreasing in the last few years. The National Crime Victimization Survey for 1996 reported that the property and violent crime rates for that year were the lowest since the survey's inception in 1973 (Ringel 1997).

Other reports note similar trends (NCES 1998). Unfortunately, crime is far from disappearing. The new trends in national crime do not imply that streets and schools are safe again. The statistics indicate that *increases* in crime have leveled out or even slowed in the adult population, but crime still occurs much more frequently than it did in the past.

Youth demographics are important for estimating the size of the population involved in crimes. Estimates are that the number of youth under age 18 will grow by between 20% and 31% in the next decade. The "baby boom echo" and immigration will bring the school-age population from 55.3 million in 1971 to 55.9 million by year 2005. Furthermore, many of these youths will live in poverty and be left largely unsupervised. In 1998 the Census Bureau reported that child poverty rates (about 20% of all children) remain double that of adults.

Schools are facing increasing numbers of children who have been abused or neglected. Between 1986 and 1993, there was an 82% rise in sexual abuse, a 102% rise in physical neglect, a 333% rise in emotional neglect, and a 42% rise in physical abuse among children. The number of students who suffered serious injury from maltreatment rose 299% between 1986 and 1993 (Sedlak and Broadhurst 1996).

Geographic Variations

Violence is not limited to urban areas; it now is common in rural and suburban schools. A recent study in rural Tennessee details 229 violent acts committed by students toward teachers in the 27 high schools responding to questionnaires; these attacks included one murder, two armed robberies, one reported rape, 129 acts of vandalism, 86 threats against teachers, one arson, and nine cases of physical violence (Duhon-Sells 1995). Incidents in suburban towns in Massachusetts, in small towns in Texas, and in rural areas in Kentucky, New York, and California led Bill Martin, spokesman for the National Education Association, to conclude, "There's no geographic exclusion anymore. . . . It could happen anywhere at any time" (Lawton 1993).

6

Different geographic areas suffer from different rates of crime. Homicide rates are higher in urban areas than in rural areas. In 1995, one-third of all murders of juveniles in the United States occurred in 10 counties that contain major cities (U.S. Department of Justice 1997). The greatest difference between urban and rural crime is in the rate for robbery, which occurs 54 times more frequently to urban citizens than to rural citizens (Weisheit, Falcone, and Wells 1994). And victimization of all types continues to occur more frequently to urbanites, with an overall victimization rate of 30%, while suburbanites suffer about 23% and rural citizens about 17% victimization rates. Unfortunately, urban-style violence — often driven by urban drug trafficking — is spreading into suburban and rural areas.

Different geographic areas also suffer from different types of crime. In rural areas, homicide, rape, and assault are more likely to occur among acquaintances than is true in urban areas. In addition, when urban-style violence spreads into rural areas, it can combine in particularly deadly ways with the traditional rural mistrust of government and the reticence to display emotions or share burdens (Weisheit, Falcone, and Wells 1994).

In rural areas, however, the traditional forms of social control can reinforce crime-prevention efforts. Teachers, business and civic leaders, clergy, and the elderly may be instrumental in reinforcing community values and holding youth to local mores.

While rural areas still claim an edge on safety, the reduction of violence in urban areas is a notable achievement resulting from years of careful analysis and prevention efforts by criminologists, public officials, and community activists. Apparently, a mix of general community policing techniques and social work dramatically decreases the level of crime on our streets. These methods can be applied to all schools, urban, rural, and suburban.

Of course, many tragedies result from the perennial teenage problems of romantic jealousy, depression, anger, and loneliness, made deadlier by the presence of guns. It was not drugs, gangs, or poverty that changed the rural town of Grayson, Kentucky, when a shy, 17-year-old honor student strode into his English class and shot and killed his 48-year-old English teacher. He also killed the janitor who came to her assistance, and he held the rest of the class hostage in a manner reminiscent of a scene in the Stephen King novel, *Rage*, which the youth had just read. Apparently, Scott Pennington's cries for help after a disturbing move from another state had gone unheeded. His self-worth plunged, his love of the macabre grew, and his admiration of Stephen King became worship.

It also was not drugs or gangs that caused an 11-year-old and a 13-year-old boy to murder four girls and a teacher and to wound 11 others during a midday ambush at the Westside Middle School in Jonesboro, Arkansas. Nor did gangs cause a 14-year-old to kill a teacher and wound another teacher and two pupils at an eighth-grade graduation dance in Edinboro, Pennsylvania.

These crimes were caused by individual problems, and it was the easy availability of guns that made them possible. That is another danger in rural areas, where guns are carried in pickups as commonly as are flashlights, fishing poles, and mud boots.

Perceptions of the Danger

Americans, from school-age children to superintendents, feel increasingly vulnerable. This is true regardless of the geographic area in which they live. Recent surveys reveal that youth fear violent crime more than any other concern, unveiling "a portrait of a generation living in fear. The security of their parents' generation and the optimistic view of the future, is no longer taken for granted. . . . For them, the poll found, the American Dream may be dying" (Ingrassia 1993).

While this fear is real, it often does not match reality. Some students express more fear than is warranted by their local situation. That is especially true for children who are exposed to a great deal of violence in the media. On the other hand, students who live in neighborhoods where murder and other forms of violence are common, and who are exposed to high levels of violence in the media, may come to see such violence as "normal." Those children may have less fear than is warranted in their environments.

Self-perceptions among adults may not be much more accurate than among children and youth. When the *Executive Educator* polled school leaders across the nation on trends in violence in their districts, discrepancies were found between the violence administrators observed in their own districts and what they reported for neighboring districts. For example, out of 1,216 responses from elementary principals, 47% thought school violence had increased in their own district, 69% thought school violence increased in neighboring districts, and 97% thought school violence had increased nationally. Similarly, about 30% to 40% of middle school and high school principals thought that school violence increased in their own schools, about 50% to 60% thought violence increased in neighboring schools, and 97% to 99% thought it increased nationally (Boothe et al. 1993, p. 20).

For school administrators, school violence is an intrinsically political question (OJP 1995, p. 3). Administrators have a vested interest in showing how well they are performing in keeping schools safe, especially how well they are doing in comparison to administrators in other school districts with similar challenges. For this reason, administrators and public relations officials often project more confidence and offer better data than is justified for their schools.

Neither are teacher fears good gauges of violence. Some teachers exaggerate the incidence of violent behaviors to get administrative attention. Other teachers may feel the need to understate the problem in order to keep their jobs, to improve job performance ratings, or to avoid calling attention to themselves.

If perceptions are unreliable sources of information, is there some other way to gauge the extent of the problem? Unfortunately, the data on school violence are not very reliable. For example, a 1989 Justice Department survey found that 7% of rural and suburban students claimed they were victims of violence or that they feared violence in their schools. This figure is just 1% less than for urban students, which would give the impression that overall crime rates are similar for rural, suburban, and urban populations. That is not the case.

Several factors make it difficult to collect reliable data on school violence from students. Perhaps the most important factor is students' reluctance to report being victimized. There is reason to believe that students do not report it when they have been assaulted, bullied, or threatened with a gun. In a recent survey of rural and urban students, 68% said they prefer to settle arguments among themselves after school. Only about 11% of students go to school officials for help, and about 22% do not know what to do. Only about 50% of victims believe that principals should be told when a fight occurs; most students do not expect help, justice, or protection from school administrators. To the question, "Students who fight in school should be punished by teachers and principals — yes or no?" only 9% said "yes" (Haberman and Dill 1995).

Another factor is how administrators handle the reports they do receive from students. Reporting data on violence is almost always tied to some incentive system. For example, if reporting these incidents supports local lobbying efforts for a bond to build a new alternative school, the incentive is to report. On the other hand, if school board elections or administrators' jobs are at stake, the incentive may be to deflate the number of incidents reported. In addition, administrator reports are not reliable indicators of the types of crime committed in schools. For example, while school administrators generally express concern about gang-related incidents at school, their reports seldom indicate whether school crimes are, in fact, gang motivated (Goldstein and Huff 1993).

Competing agendas are not the only problem affecting the accuracy of data about school violence. The lack of a uniform definition of violence also confounds efforts to keep schools safe. What constitutes a violent incident? Is name-calling violent? Harassment? Bullying? Pushing? Threatening with a water pistol? Threatening with a pen knife? While precise definitions may seem like insignificant sticking points in a discussion of something as serious as school violence, precision is, in fact, crucially important. Accurate reporting of violent incidents depends on a uniform and universally accepted definition of what constitutes an "incident." Such definitions also clarify the expectations about what is acceptable behavior.

The problems with defining and reporting school violence result in a melange of often contradictory statistics. For example, in 1995 the National Center for Education Statistics reported that victimization rates of high school seniors changed little between 1976 and 1993, with the single exception of a rise in weapon threats. Those results conflict with a survey conducted by the National Association of State Boards of Education the year before. In the NASBE survey, only half of the students surveyed reported feeling "very safe" in school, and nearly one-fourth said they had been victimized by violence either inside or near their school (NASBE 1994, p. 9).

Educators and policy makers need reliable information to solve the problem of school violence. Fortunately, several organizations have focused on gathering reliable, comprehensive data on school violence. Among these organizations are the National Institute of Justice, an office of the U.S. Department of Justice; the National School Safety Center (NSSC) in Encino, California; and the Metropolitan Life Insurance Company Survey.

Defining Violence

The failure of educators to agree on a definition for school violence has serious consequences. Not only does it confound the collection of data, but it also results in their overlooking a variety of intrinsically aggressive acts. That is the "boys will be boys" syndrome, in which educators accept bullying, pushing, name-calling, teasing, offensive gestures, and other derogatory behaviors. These "lesser" offenses are the roots of school violence.

So what is violence? The Study Group of the National Association of State Boards of Education defined violence as "any condition or situation that creates actual or fear of physical, psychological, or emotional harm and therefore impedes learning" (NASBE 1994). The American Psychological Association has put forth a similar definition: "Violence refers to immediate or chronic situations that result in injury to the psychological, social, or physical well-being of individuals or groups" (1993, p. 1). The definition used by the Johnson Institute helps educators focus on non-physical as well as physical harm: "Violence occurs whenever anyone inflicts or threatens to inflict physical or emotional injury or discomfort upon another person's body, feelings, or possessions." Translated into a child's language, violence would be "any mean word, look, sign, or act that hurts a person's body, feelings, or things" (Remboldt 1994, p. 5).

Many researchers consider violence to be a public health issue, defining it as a threat that is no less virulent than polio, tuberculosis, or AIDS. In *Deadly Consequences*, Deborah Prothrow-Stith provides a very pragmatic explanation of this approach: "To me a problem that destroys health by causing so much injury and death is a health problem" (1991, p. 28).

Regarding school violence as a health problem provides schools with a model for dealing with the problem. In the same way that schools have provided children with immunizations against diseases and information about the dangers of smoking and drunk driving, they now can teach students to solve problems nonviolently. This public health definition of violence is empowering; it assumes there is at least one thing the schools can do.

The Price of Fear

An atmosphere of fear pervades many schools. This fear is most prevalent in urban environments, particularly in urban schools where a majority of the students are poor or people of color. But fear is not limited to those schools.

Fear may vary throughout the school day and may differ in various parts of the school building. Vulnerability increases with isolation, so that arriving early or staying late causes greater anxiety. Students feel more vulnerable in isolated parts of the building, such as locker rooms and bathrooms. Areas of concern for students rank approximately as follows: 1) hallways and staircases, 2) locker rooms, 3) boys' then girls' bathrooms, 4) the gymnasium, and 5) classrooms (Louis Harris and Associates 1993).

Students' fears often are justified. Nearly one-third of all students have witnessed violence in and around their schools; 6% witness violence often. Student conversations about violence at school are increasingly common, with as many as 55% of all students discussing violence either very often or occasionally (Louis Harris and Associates 1993).

The pervasive fear among our students is a critical problem for our nation. By itself, fear is incendiary and may lead to violence. In addition, the future stability of our nation's youth is greatly jeopardized by childhoods never grounded in security or safety. Students' fears affect their ability to focus on learning. Their fears may cause students to carry a gun or knife for protection, or students may self-medicate their anxiety with alcohol and drugs. And a significant number of students will react to fear by becoming aggressive and volatile themselves.

Fear also can result in emotional isolation. That is especially true for children who live in poor neighborhoods, where drugs, prostitution, and drive-by shootings are common. It is not safe for youths in those neighborhoods to "hang out" with their friends in the community, but it also is psychologically detrimental for them to stay inside alone. As Prothrow-Stith notes, adolescents in poverty must "choose between survival and their developmentally-compelled need for age-mates" (1991, p. 90).

To deal successfully with daily life in an often-violent neighborhood, children and adolescents require someone who cares about them and who is able to help them process their feelings and experiences. If this is not available, youths can become callous to brutality. Unfortunately, children are deserted and neglected too often. In "The Children's Roundtable," sponsored by the Carnegie Corporation, former congressman Thomas Downey asserted, "In the past three decades, we have gone from two-parent families to one-parent families to, alarmingly, an extraordinary incidence of no-parent families" (Downey 1993). Because these children feel vulnerable, they parade a "macho" image and may carry guns to enforce that image. They also may numb themselves to violence in order to survive psychologically.

The Roots of Violence

Educators must understand the causes of school violence if they are going to implement programs to stop it. There is a fairly large industry devoted to school safety, including consultants and staff developers, books and videotapes, each touting one or more programs to deal with the problem. Different groups of stakeholders call for conflict-resolution training, metal detectors, security police, transparent backpacks, and other strategies for dealing with violent students. If educators are to choose the strategies that are appropriate for their school, they must be able to evaluate the factors that combine to produce violent behavior in their particular setting.

Despite some increasing interest in the biological underpinnings for crime, scientists generally accept that the high availability of guns, economic inequity, and a violence-saturated culture and media — none of which are caused by heredity — are the striking features of a violence-prone landscape. Reiss and Roth note that "Modern psychological perspectives emphasize that aggressive and violent behaviors are *learned* responses to frustration, and that they can also be learned as instruments for achieving goals, and that the learning occurs by observing models of such behavior" (1993, p. 7).

Level of education, IQ, racial or ethnic characteristics, and similar variables are poor predictors of crime rates. Instead, poverty is the prime predictor for both aggressive behavior and victimization. As the percent of households below the poverty level per census tract increases, so does the homicide rate (Reiss and Roth 1993). However, while poverty is correlated with violence, it is not a cause of violence. Rather, poverty and its effect on family cohesion may lower "social capital." Chronic poverty often precipitates such risk factors as maternal depression, lowered expectations, household disorganization, eating few or no meals together, and others. Violence emerges from the absence of positive social interactions and the presence of sinister models in the same way that empathy emerges from social interaction and reconciliation in a healthy human society (Duncan, Dunifon, and Doran 1998).

14

Poverty breaks down the formal and informal social systems that serve to regulate behavior (Reiss and Roth 1993). It is the absence of these norms that breeds chaos and violence. This effect is greatly multiplied by the easy accessibility of guns. Few children admit to carrying weapons with a premeditated plan to use them against specific targets. Instead, the gun serves as a form of protection for the child who feels unprotected by parents, teachers, police, church, or any other social institution and whose diminished self-esteem often results from growing up oppressed (Kozol 1991).

While poverty is a prime predictor of violence, antisocial behavior is not limited to only the poor. Indeed, a number of children from economically advantaged homes also are suffering from parental neglect. Some of the factors associated with youth violence include intergenerational antisocial behavior, marital conflict, divorce, unemployment, poor disciplinary methods, parental rejection, parental criminality and aggressiveness, and poor parental health, as well as child abuse and neglect (Goldstein and Huff 1993).

Televised violence also may influence youth violence. Television viewing occupies an increasingly large amount of many students' nonschool hours. Poor youths watch more television than those who are in higher socioeconomic groups (Prothrow-Stith 1991). African-American youth are "voracious consumers of nonprint media . . . watching about 77 hours of television a week, about 50% more than the average for other groups" (Schmidt 1993). Children between the ages of two and five years watch about 28 hours of television weekly — more time than is spent in any other activity except sleeping. And the above figures do not include the time spent watching recorded programs on a VCR, which involves about two-thirds of all television watchers (Nielsen Media Research 1990).

By the time a child graduates from high school, he or she will have seen no less than 18,000 television murders and 800 suicides (National Center for Injury Prevention 1989). That relentless media violence contributes to the violence in real life (NAEYC 1990). The use of violence as a way to solve problems is actively encouraged by many television shows, some of which also advertise toy weapons. The American Psychological Association, in fact, avers that "television itself may be responsible for one-half of all homicides nationally" (Bender 1993). The introduction of television alone into a community that formerly did not have the medium doubles the homicide rate within a 10- to 15-year period (Vooijs and van der Voort 1993).

The Centers for Disease Control and Prevention notes that, "Research in the last twenty years has repeatedly found an association between media violence and aggressive behavior, often linked to viewers' perceptions of television reality and their identification with television characters" (Hendrix and Molloy 1990). Until the age of seven or eight, about second or third grade, children cannot distinguish between reality and fantasy (NAEYC 1990). Hendrix and Molloy note that when young children believe that television represents real life and when aggression is rewarded and considered appropriate in lifelike TV shows, the effect is to escalate violence and increase the viewers' callousness or apathy toward others. Children get used to violence and eventually come to enjoy vicious behavior, a process known as "habituation" (Hendrix and Molloy 1990).

Many children may believe that watching television is the only option they have. However, educators can help children generate numerous other options, many of which will contribute to school achievement. Students also can be taught to observe the level of violence in television programming, which may raise their awareness of the effects of the shows they watch.

References

American Psychological Association. *Violence and Youth: Psychology's Response*. Washington, D.C., 1993.

Bastian, L. "Criminal Victimization 1993." *Bureau of Justice Statistics National Crime Victimization Survey Bulletin* (May 1995).

Bender, N.S. "An Epidemic of Violence." *ATPE News* 13 (January/February 1993): 14-16.

Boothe, J.W.; Bradley, L.H.; Flick, M.T.; Keough, K.; and Kirk, S. "The Violence at Your Door." *Executive Educator* 15 (February 1993): 20.

Downey, T. "Toward a New Future for America's Children." *Urban Institute Update* (April 1993): 2.

Duhon-Sells, Rose, ed. *Dealing with Youth Violence*. Bloomington, Ind.: National Educational Service, 1995.

Duncan, G.; Dunifon, R.; and Doran, M. "How Different Are Welfare and Working Families?" Paper prepared for the conference of the Joint Center for Poverty Research, Chicago, May 1998.

Goldstein, A., and Huff, C.R. *The Gang Intervention Handbook*. Champaign, Ill.: Research Press, 1993.

Haberman, M., and Dill, V. "Commitment to Violence Among Teenagers in Poverty." *Kappa Delta Pi Record* 31 (Summer 1995): 148-56.

Hendrix, K., and Molloy, P. *Interventions in Early Childhood*. Atlanta: Centers for Disease Control and the Minority Health Professions Foundation with the Morehouse School of Medicine, 1990.

Ingrassia, M. "Growing Up Fast and Frightened." *Newsweek*, 22 November 1993, p. 52.

Kozol, J. *Savage Inequalities: Children in America's Schools*. New York: Crown, 1991.

Lawton, M. "Officials Remove Two from School Because Father Is Seen as Threat." *Education Week*, 26 May 1993, p. 5.

Levine, Arthur, and Nidiffer, Jana. *Beating the Odds: How the Poor Get to College*. San Francisco: Jossey-Bass, 1996.

Louis Harris and Associates. *The Metropolitan Life Survey of the American Teacher: Violence in America's Public Schools*. New York, 1993.

National Association for the Education of Young Children (NAEYC). "Position Statement on Media Violence in Children's Lives." *Young Children* 45, no. 5 (1990): 17-21.

National Association of State Boards of Education (NASBE). *Report of the NASBE Study Group on Violence and Its Impact on Schools and Learning*. Alexandria, Va., October 1994.

National Center for Education Statistics. *Violence and Discipline Problems in the U.S. Public Schools: 1996-97*. Washington, D.C.: U.S. Department of Education, 1998.

National Center for Education Statistics. *The Condition of Education, 1995*. Washington, D.C.: U.S. Department of Education, 1995.

National Center for Injury Prevention and Control. *The Prevention of Youth Violence: A Framework for Community Action.* Atlanta: Centers for Disease Control and Prevention, 1989.

Nielsen Media Research. "1990 Report on Television." Northbrook, Ill.: A.C. Nielsen, 1990.

Office of Justice Programs (OJP). *Weapon-Related Victimization in Selected Inner-City High School Samples.* Washington, D.C.: U.S. Department of Justice, February 1995.

Prothrow-Stith, Deborah. *Deadly Consequences: How Violence Is Destroying Our Teenage Population and a Plan to Begin Solving the Problem.* New York: HarperCollins, 1991.

Reiss, A., and Roth, J. *Understanding and Preventing Violence.* Washington, D.C.: National Academy Press, 1993.

Remboldt, C. *Violence in Schools: The Enabling Factor.* Minneapolis: Johnson Institute, 1994.

Ringel, Cheryl. "Criminal Victimization 1996: Changes 1995-96 with Trends 1993-96." *Bureau of Justice Statistics National Crime Victimization Survey Bulletin* (November 1997).

Rugg, Carol D. *A Fine Line: Losing American Youth to Violence.* Flint, Mich.: Charles Stewart Mott Foundation, 1995.

Schmidt, P. "Symposium Urges Youth Agencies to Be 'Hip' to City Teenagers." *Education Week,* 10 March 1993, p. 5.

"School Shooting Leaves Three Dead." *Executive Educator* 18 (March 1996): 8.

Sedlak, A., and Broadhurst, D. *Executive Summary of the Third National Incidence Study of Child Abuse and Neglect.* Washington, D.C.: U.S. Department of Health and Human Services; Administration for Children and Families; Administration on Children, Youth and Families; and National Center on Child Abuse and Neglect, September 1996.

Sheley, J.; McGee, Z.; and Wright, J. *Weapon-Related Victimization in Selected Inner-City High School Samples.* National Institute of Justice Research Report NCJ151526. Washington, D.C.: U.S. Department of Justice, February 1995.

U.S. Department of Commerce. "Poverty Rate Down, Household Income Up — Both Return to 1989 Pre-Recession Levels." Press release. Washington, D.C., 24 September 1998.

U.S. Department of Justice. *Juvenile Offenders and Victims: 1997 Update on Violence.* Washington, D.C., 1997.

Vooijs, M., and van der Voort, Tom. "Learning About Television Violence: The Impact of a Critical Viewing Curriculum on Children's Attitudinal Judgments of Crime Series." *Journal of Research and Development in Education* 26 (Spring 1993):133-42.

Weisheit, R.; Falcone, D.; and Wells, L.E. "Rural Crime and Rural Policing." National Institute of Justice Newsletter (October 1994): 2.

Whitman, David. "Is Lack of Money the Reason Kids Stay Poor?" *U.S. News and World Report*, 2 June 1997, p. 33.

Chapter Two

Dysfunctional Schools

Because, in our society, violence often is accepted as "normal," schools must be counter-cultural institutions. Educators must resist societal violence on a daily basis; they must create "safe havens" where children feel comfortable, confident, and relaxed enough to learn. In order to accomplish these things, educators must attend to two related efforts:

- Educators must become aware of and eliminate the factors by which schools and individuals unintentionally increase the likelihood of violence.
- They must make visible, conscious efforts to ensure safety at all levels and in all areas of the building.

Unfortunately, a school that appears to be clean, orderly, and safe may, quite unintentionally, foster violence. Some of the factors that lead to violence are brought to the school by the students, but others are caused by the faculty or by the institutional culture of the school. Usually, various factors combine to cause violence. Some of the problems brought to school by the students are:

- Gang activity
- Emotional problems
- A belief that one is "entitled" to be violent

Many of the problems that students bring to the school are well known. Gangs, for example, have received a great deal of attention in both the popular and professional press. Not only do gangs lead directly to violence as they compete for "turf," their presence also exacerbates the free-floating anger that may be present in a school. Some of the more obvious indications that gangs are operating in a school are:

- Gangs have been present in the community in the past.
- Groups of students congregate by racial identity, occasionally calling their group a name that would solidify their identity ("The Red Rozes," "The Perfect Perils," etc.).
- There is an increasing number of violent, racially based incidents.
- The rate of absenteeism is increasing, and crimes in the community increasingly are committed by truants.
- Graffiti and crossed-out graffiti are visible on or near the school.
- Colors are worn symbolically by various groups who also employ hand signals and wear unique symbols on T-shirts or in jewelry.
- Students carry beepers, cell phones, or pagers, suggesting that drugs are available in or around the school.

When a school has a gang problem, teachers and principals need ongoing technical assistance. They must learn how to avoid a show-down that pits student against teacher or student against principal in a bid for peer approval. And teachers need to understand the "triggers" for violent behavior and must demonstrate their commitment to resolving conflicts and incidents peacefully.

Educators often forget how important it is for students to feel respected. Unless each student feels respected — according to the student's definition of respect — by both authority figures and peers, some form of violence is almost inevitable.

Normal adolescent development includes periods of intense self-doubt and rebellion. However, among poor children and those who are not succeeding academically, these feelings can be particularly severe. Theirs is a fragile world in which survival requires wearing a mask of intimidation that makes them feel strong, worthy, or popular. Students with extremely low self-esteem often are unreasonably vigilant or quick-tempered about the many ways in which other people, both teachers and students, may offend them. Educators who ignore this hyper-vigilance are contributing to the danger in their schools.

In addition, schools often fail to recognize the early signs of risk for violence in children. Even at a very young age, violent children set themselves apart from other children in ways that make their problems worse. While educators often recognize these children, their responses may inadvertently exacerbate the problem.

For example, young children who are going through a family crisis may become aggressive at school. Teachers often respond to this behavior by isolating the child in "time out." Unfortunately, teachers often place these students in isolation for increasingly long periods of time in an effort to stop a behavior that the isolation is making worse. In persistent cases, the child is transferred to another class or school, which further exacerbates the problem. Eventually the child may be placed in a special education setting for emotionally disturbed children.

For very young children, disruptive classroom behavior tends to contribute to poor relationships with friends; that, in turn, contributes to ongoing problems at school, low self-esteem, and more violent behavior (American Psychological Association 1993). A vicious cycle is started.

Often what is needed is not isolation, but counseling, personal attention, and self-esteem building while, at the same time, teaching the child that his or her aggressive behavior is simply unacceptable.

Another problem that students bring to the school is really a social or cultural problem. That is, many students feel that they are "entitled" to respond violently. The belief that violence is a normal response to any provocation often is reinforced by adults who never challenge that assumption. Too often, adults respond to minor violent incidents by saying that "boys will be boys" or "I went through that when I was her age." That adult response can contribute greatly to the problem of school violence (Canada 1995).

How Schools Encourage Violence

The school itself often creates conditions that contribute to violent behavior. The actions of individual educators, school policies, and the general climate of a school all can increase tensions, and thus also increase the likelihood of violence. Some of the problems caused by school climate or by individual faculty include:

- Failing to challenge all manifestations of violence
- Not having a plan or vision for school safety
- Tracking
- High failure rates
- Using suspensions and expulsions to control behavior
- Mandatory transfers of "problem" students
- Use of corporal punishment and humiliation
- Crowding
- Authoritarian rules with quick punishment

Many schools have no plan or vision for preventing violence. Each teacher is left to deal with potentially violent situations in whatever way he or she chooses. One teacher may humiliate students who misbehave, another teacher may simply kick them out of class. A few teachers may attempt to keep aggressive students in class and work to change their behaviors. And other teachers may feel powerless to confront aggressive or violent students.

Unclear thinking and lack of vision have led school boards and administrators to some bizarre "solutions." At one time, transparent plastic backpacks were marketed by clever companies as an answer to school violence. It should have taken only a few minutes for educators to realize that knives, guns, and drugs can be wrapped in gym clothes, hidden in folders, or brought through open windows. The bags, the gimmicks, the mirrors, and the quick fixes seldom work; and parents usually foot the bill for these silly solutions.

As bad as having no plan can be, it can be much worse to have a simplistic, authoritarian policy. Especially in the current political climate, it seems easy just to punish offenders and punish them hard. Three strikes! Zero tolerance! As soon as children step a little out of line, crack down on them instantly. There are many rules, all supported by coercion. Students frequently are suspended or expelled. Or even worse, the school frequently uses corporal punishment, thus teaching the students that violence is an appropriate way to get what one wants.

On the other hand, a well-thought-out plan, collaboratively developed, can help prevent violence. Such a plan should include input from students about what they think and know about their own safety. The plan should describe the attitudes and values that not only will build the foundation for a safe school but will serve the students throughout their lives. In addition, the plan should balance students' rights to privacy with their needs for safety and an effective education.

A well-thought-out plan will concern more than just how to control the students. It also will affect the school's curriculum and teaching methods. For example, homogeneous grouping, or "tracking," has considerable implications for school safety. Students who are from the same neighborhoods and who share a particular socioeconomic status often are tracked together. Such tracking strengthens the cliques formed outside of school and further divides the student body. In that way, homogeneous grouping can make the violence that occurs outside of school more difficult to challenge inside school.

Tracking also divides students into winners and losers. It ensures that students in the vocational and remedial classes do not experience the values and attitudes of students who are in the college-bound track. Students in the lower tracks do not experience the high expectations of teachers who gear their instruction so their students can go on to college. Instead, tracking reinforces peer values for each track, brands those in the lower tracks as losers, and pits those losers against the school's winners.

Schools that use tracking are organized in such a way that "losers and dropouts" are easily identified by their schedules. Tracking also makes racial stereotyping, racial slurs, and outright discrimination easier ("Don't take that class; it's all geeks," or "Fundamentals of Math! That's for wetbacks!"). Indeed, such schools are the first, unwitting organizers of youth gangs.

On the other hand, schools that use mixed-ability grouping demonstrate that individuals who are quite different in interests and abilities still can communicate, learn together, cooperate, and complete tasks that all consider to be important. Mixed-ability groups build skills that are needed in the real world, where people differ dramatically but must still work together to complete tasks. Most important for young people who are in danger of failing school, mixed-ability groups eliminate the stigma of remedial classes, allow the possibility that positive values and attitudes toward learning can spread to at-risk youth, give all youth the high expectations often reserved just for the college-bound, and sometimes lead teachers to recognize talent where they did not expect to find it. Mixed-ability classes appear to serve all students well (Chase and Doan 1994).

The current "standards movement" also poses a danger to schools. High expectations are wonderful, but high standards often are a very different thing. Currently, the term "high standards" has been used by school boards, state lawmakers, and other political groups to mean narrowly defined education targets assessed by standardized tests. These groups demand that all children meet these standards, but rarely are the children given the support needed to succeed.

As school becomes less interesting and more irritating to students, they are more likely to lose hope, fail a grade, or drop out. Failing a grade lowers a youth's self-esteem and increases the likelihood that he or she will lash out at school or schoolmates (Dill nd). In order to feel better about themselves, such youths may spend a lifetime escaping into drugs or trying to sabotage others' success. They become a grave danger to themselves, their school, and their community.

If numerous children in a school are failing, it is a signal that it is the school itself that is failing. Such a school is in danger of becoming increasingly violent. Students who fail a grade will try to regain their self-respect by demanding respect from others, often by bullying weaker students. When large numbers of stu-

26

dents must take remedial classes — especially when those remedial classes seem to be characterized along ethnic or racial lines — these students may pose a danger to all students. That does not mean that students must be passed from one grade to the next regardless of the work they do for their classes. But there are many approaches to decrease the number of students who flunk a grade or class (see Chapter Five). The more of these programs that are in place in a school, the more likely it will be that this school's students will feel good about themselves, will not be bored or excessively frustrated in class, and will not value violence as a means to achieve respect.

A school's suspension and expulsion policy also may increase the level of violence. These policies usually are based on four questionable assumptions:

1. The student wants to be in school and will regard expulsion as a punishment.
2. The student's family or parents will do a better job of controlling the student after the suspension or expulsion and will be a source of criticism that the student will fear and respect.
3. The student's peers will increase the sense of shame the student feels at being suspended and this will make the student behave better in the future.
4. Being denied the privilege of an education for a short period of time will itself be educational. Students so value their education that fear of suspension will cause them to behave less violently in the future.

Of course, none of these assumptions is valid. Instead, suspensions and expulsions have unintended consequences that defeat the school's educational purpose for using them:

1. Being out of school is a reward.
2. Parents and family are likely to support the youth's perception that the suspension or expulsion was unfair and discriminatory.
3. Peers are likely to admire a friend who is suspended.

4. Because the suspension fails to have the intended effect on the student, the student realizes that school has no effective means for teaching the less violent behaviors it regards as desirable.

What the expulsion teaches some students is that violent behavior can accomplish good things for those students perpetrating it, including gaining approval from peers and possibly even from family members.

There is a more worthwhile reason for using suspensions and expulsions. These strategies often are used to protect other students and teachers from the students who are considered dangerous. However, these strategies do not solve the problem of violence. Violent students often desire to be kicked out of school, so the threat of expulsion actually encourages the student to be violent. In addition, these strategies put the students into the neighborhood where, research indicates, they are likely to commit illegal acts (Goldstein and Huff 1993). And because the level of crime and violence in a neighborhood affects the level of violence in a school, administrators who use suspensions and expulsions have merely hidden the problem, not solved it.

Schools that commonly use suspension and expulsion are dysfunctional. Such schools have abandoned their mission to teach difficult students, finding it much easier to expel them than to gain their cooperation. These schools also have set up an adversarial atmosphere in which students are kept in line with threats and punishments. Something is desperately wrong with schools that continue the same ineffective "discipline strategy" over and over despite the fact that it is a disadvantage to the students and to the community.

Similarly, there is no evidence that corporal punishment is an effective discipline strategy. According to data supplied by the U.S. Department of Education Office of Civil Rights, 470,683 students were subjected to corporal punishment during the 1993-94 school year. Twenty-seven states now ban corporal punishment of any kind; 23 allow it. In Texas, every year 114,213 children receive corporal punishment, with African-American students significantly overrepresented among the victims (CED 1998). Of the 470,683 reported incidents throughout the nation, approximately 31,000 were disabled students (AAP 1998). Fortunately, incidents of corporal punishment seem to be declining.

The American Academy of Pediatrics, the American Medical Association, and forty other major national organizations favor abolition of corporal punishment. Research indicates that corporal punishment is especially damaging to children who are neglected or abused. Known side-effects of corporal punishment include aggression, vandalism, lowered school achievement, poor attention span, increases in dropout rates, school phobias, depression, suicide, and violence against teachers (Poole et al. 1991).

Three patterns seem to apply in schools where paddling or some other form of corporal punishment is common:

1. Minorities and the youngest students are beaten most frequently
2. The same students are beaten repeatedly.
3. There is no evidence to link corporal punishment with decreases in disruptive behavior or increases in learning (Haberman and Dill 1994).

The lesson of corporal punishment is that it is acceptable to beat others into submission. Unfortunately, many violent children have seldom or never witnessed any alternative to violence in their homes or neighborhoods. They have never seen, studied, or talked about other types of behavior. Schools that use corporal punishment confirm the students' belief that there is no alternative to hitting, forcing, humiliating, and violating others.

Another sign of a dysfunctional school is one that educators usually cannot control: crowding. High numbers of students crowded into a limited space increase the likelihood of violence (American Psychological Association 1993). Packing large numbers of students into crowded halls, ill-lit portable buildings or trailers, or tight classroom quarters begs for trouble.

While educators cannot force their communities to build more school buildings, there are strategies they can use to reduce the effects of crowding. For example, schedules can be arranged to stagger changes between classes so that hundreds of students do not pour into the halls simultaneously. There also are strategies for reducing class sizes and finding adequate classroom space for large classes, such as extending the school day.

Finally, researchers have isolated the "triggers" that make kids angry and lead to violence. While one or two of these triggers may not cause severe problems, having many of them in one school will greatly increase the tension in the school and increase the likelihood of violence. These triggers include:

1. Closed campuses.
2. Teachers may smoke in the presence of students, who may not.
3. Inadequate time to pass between classes.
4. Dress codes.
5. "Dressing out" requirements for physical education (Kadel and Follman 1993, p. 61).

"Dance of the Lemons"

In some cities, it is common practice to transfer students with behavior disorders to other schools, which often euphemistically is termed the "dance of the lemons." The school that ejects the students may then claim it has a zero suspension and expulsion rate, because mandatory transfers do not "count." This is a hypocritical — and dangerous — public relations ploy.

The schools that receive these students often do not know why the student was transferred. Mandatory record disclosure laws vary from state to state; and the students records, including parole conditions or police records, may not be accessible. The practice creates an absolute danger for the receiving school.

Transferring violent students from one school or district to another benefits no one except the administrators of the sending school. While the policy may supply the student with a "fresh start," it does so by removing the continuity of understanding from counselors, teachers, or other support personnel who can provide long-term help to the student to change his or her behavior permanently. Further, it adds to an already violent student's life the trauma of moving to a new situation where new relationships must be established, perhaps with bullish behavior or dangerous displays of brute force. Less violent students are hardly helped by this dubious approach, and violent students are not held accountable for their own behavior.

When there is stability in the school lives of students, when all the students in a school are known by the teachers, there is less school crime. Every student can build a relationship with teachers and counselors. The practice of transferring violent students has the opposite effect. It implies that this student is not worth getting to know.

Another policy is to send violent students to alternative schools. Most of these alternative programs have the goal of eventually returning the students to the regular school, but many of these alternative schools really act as "warehouses" to hold the students until they drop out.

There are innovative and successful alternative schools for violent students. These schools coordinate social, medical, and educational services to provide counseling, remediation, and mentors to help the students to a successful completion of a diploma or GED. These successful alternative schools have some important lessons for regular schools. Unfortunately, few alternative schools for violent students are successful.

Guidelines for Safety

Students can learn more acceptable behavior, despite poor models at home, a brutalizing culture, and many years of antisocial behavior. But these students need teachers who are willing to expend the empathy and perseverance needed to build relationships with youth.

Educators need to be aware of the safety problems in their schools, and they need to plan to solve these problems. In addi-

31

tion, any violence prevention plan should be articulated across grade levels and schools, from kindergarten through high school. The same vocabulary, procedures, program, and models should be present in each school to help students make a smooth transition into a new environment.

Every school should have guidelines and committees already in place to deal with issues of school safety. School safety committees should look at a variety of factors that are present in their schools and develop plans for dealing with unexpected situations. Some of the questions such a committee should consider are:

1. Is there a local school security committee or task force composed of school administrators, law enforcement personnel, youth counselors, parents, and students to plan the safety measures needed and to regularly review school safety and security measures?

2. Do the principals possess "crime-resistance savvy" and take full responsibility in working with the school board and district to ensure that school safety and emergency contingency plans are in place?

3. What type of communication network does the school have and how well does it work? Does it link classrooms, playgrounds, physical education sites, and all areas in which students and staff may be present to local police and fire agencies?

4. Are school staff regularly informed about safety plans through inservice training? Does the training include part-time staff, substitutes, classified staff, and all individuals who regularly visit the building and deal with students?

5. Do parents and community volunteers help patrol the surrounding neighborhoods and do they help supervise the campus before, during, and after school?

6. Are points of entry to school grounds and buildings limited and monitored during the school day? A single visitor entrance should be supervised by a receptionist or security officer; visitors should sign in and wear an identification

pass. Delivery and vendor entrances should be monitored carefully and checked regularly.

7. Has the committee considered information from the students concerning which parts of the building pose particular dangers? Do stairwells or doorways provide hiding places for dangerous activities? Are certain locations on the playground flash points for violence? Could shrubs and bushes outside the building hide intruders or weapons?

8. Are students taught to take responsibility for their own safety by reporting suspicious individuals or unusual activities on the school grounds and by learning personal safety and conflict-resolution techniques? What avenues exist for students to report possible or impending fights and yet still remain unidentified?

9. Is there a curriculum committee that focuses on teaching students nonviolence, prosocial skills, conflict resolution, law-related education, and good decision-making?

10. Should an incident occur, has the school developed a comprehensive crisis management plan involving community agencies and resources?

If the answer to more than one or two of the above questions is "no," then there could be a serious safety problem for that school. The questions were adapted from recommendations from the National School Safety Center (1990) and can be used as a checklist for overall school safety.

In response to a series of school shootings, President Clinton requested the U.S. Departments of Education and Justice to compile a guide to help educators stop troubled youths from killing others at school. That guide, *Early Warning, Timely Response: A Guide to Safe Schools* (Dwyer, Osher, and Warger 1998) focuses on helping educators to recognize the "early warning signs" that may signal that troubled youth may become violent. The report also details principles for developing prevention and intervention plans. Unfortunately, the report has a frustratingly theoretical orientation and does not address the real barriers that educators face in trying to implement such programs. Although well worth reading, the report provides little insight into specific ways to prevent violence.

Summary

Schools can be safe. However, armed guards, metal detectors, transparent backpacks, and other simplistic solutions are not the answer.

There are many approaches, programs, and solutions that have been demonstrated over time to significantly reduce the threat of school violence. Some of these solutions should be present in every school; others should be used only when they fit the needs of a particular school. What is most important is that adults be united in not permitting violence of any kind in the school. Educators can educate themselves about school safety and violence prevention. Parents can become involved in ways that will support the school and communicate to both educators and students that safety is important. Together, adults can ensure a school's safety if they make it their number-one priority. They can provide at least one place where children can be safe.

References

American Academy of Pediatrics (AAP). *Vital Issues of Corporal Punishment in Schools*. Washington, D.C., September 1998.

American Psychological Association Commission on Violence and Youth. *Violence and Youth: Psychology's Response*. New York: Sol Goldman Trust, 1993.

Canada, G. *Fist Stick Knife Gun*. Boston: Beacon Press, 1995.

Center for Effective Discipline (CED). *Facts About Corporal Punishment*. Columbus, Ohio: National Coalition to Abolish Corporal Punishment in Schools, 1998.

Chase, P., and Doan, J. *Full Circle: A New Look at Multiage Education*. Portsmouth, N.H.: Heinemann, 1994.

Dill, V. *Closing the Gap: Acceleration vs. Remediation and the Impact of Retention in Grade on Student Achievement*. Commissioner's Critical Issue Analysis Series GE3 500 02. Austin: Texas Education Agency, nd.

Dwyer, K.; Osher, D.; and Warger, C. *Early Warning, Timely Response: A Guide to Safe Schools*. Washington, D.C.: U.S. Department of Education, 1998.

Goldstein, A., and Huff, C.R. *The Gang Intervention Handbook*. Champaign, Ill.: Research Press, 1993.

Haberman, M., and Dill, V. "Can Teachers Be Educated to Save Students in a Violent Society?" In *Teachers as Leaders: Perspectives on the Professional Development of Teachers*, edited by Donovan R. Walling. Bloomington, Ind.: Phi Delta Kappa Educational Foundation, 1994.

Kadel, S., and Follman, J. *Reducing School Violence*. Tallahassee: Florida Department of Education, March 1993.

National School Safety Center. *School Crisis and Prevention*. Malibu, Calif.: Pepperdine University, March 1990.

Poole, S., et al. "The Role of the Pediatrician in Abolishing Corporal Punishment in Schools." *Pediatrics* 88 (1991): 162-67.

Chapter Three

Cultivating a
Culture of Nonviolence

Educators' beliefs affect students. That is because their beliefs are the basis for almost every decision that educators make, from their approaches to curricula to the violence prevention programs they choose (Richardson 1996). The beliefs of teachers are particularly important for preventing violence, because no other individuals in the school have more time with or influence over students than do teachers.

Teachers regularly give their students subtle and not-so-subtle messages. A teacher's beliefs about such issues as a student's worth or potential, respect, and how to solve conflicts all are communicated to students in a variety of ways. For many students — especially for those who live in poor, violent neighborhoods — their teachers' messages about resolving conflicts nonviolently may be the only such messages they receive.

It is not only teachers' beliefs about violence that affect the students. Teachers' beliefs about teaching itself may have much to do with promoting nonviolence. For example, a teacher who explores many teaching techniques to find ones that work for each student is transmitting the message, "Your success is important to me." As the student experiences success, his or her self-respect may improve. Unfortunately, some teachers' behavior reinforces the negative feelings students have. Thus teachers' beliefs can be formidable factors in nurturing a culture of peace at school.

Beliefs also drive students' behavior. Young children often directly reflect their parents' beliefs. And though adolescents frequently rebel against their parents, their oppositional behavior still is based largely on parental beliefs.

Beliefs are not the same as attitudes. An individual can have a cheerful attitude toward others while still behaving in disempowering or devastating ways. Nor is a belief the same as knowledge. Knowledge is contextual, it can be changed easily through new experiences. Beliefs are rooted in an understanding of the world; they are based on assumptions and premises, and thus can be difficult to change.

As obvious as it might seem that teacher beliefs are basic to forming school cultures that prize nonviolence, the importance of beliefs often is ignored. Instead, reformers talk about outcomes, performance, data on discipline referrals, or inventories of behaviors. When reformers ignore the reasons for keeping a school safe, they often try to educate the students merely to obey authority. When everyone in the school understands the reasons for a safe school, then the school culture educates students to build a democracy through cooperation and to gain an understanding of why decent behavior is non-negotiable. The latter approach is more likely to provide a long-term solution.

Following are eight principles that can serve as the foundation for beliefs that will lead to safer schools.

Principle One: Violence Is Not Inevitable

When we understand that violence is not inevitable, then we can learn to simply not accept violence, even in its milder manifestations. When we tolerate aggressive or violent children, we allow the behavior to continue, redefine societal norms, and motivate the children to continue testing the limits of violence.

The National Center for Injury Prevention and Control notes, "Traditionally, our society has taught us that violence often equals courage and strength. We must unlearn this tragic lesson. If we are to survive as healthy, responsible, and caring people, we must teach ourselves and our children that violence does not solve problems" (National Center for Injury Prevention and Control 1993, p. v).

There are culturally sanctioned beliefs that we must unlearn in order to establish a safe society. One is the notion that slapstick humor is funny, though the humor depends on people hurting each other. Another is the assumption that aggression is "macho" and is a prerequisite for entry into manhood. These beliefs will die hard.

It is possible to build a nonviolent society. Indeed, less than two hours from the urban, high-crime areas of Philadelphia, the Old Order Amish have built such a community. According to Donald Kraybill, a scholar of the Amish and Mennonite cultures:

> In terms of homicide rates among Amish — well, there was one just recently by a mentally sick, truly deviant Amish. . . . But homicide is, in fact, virtually nil, as are assaults. . . . These people seldom become aggressive; they may even give up their belief in God and become atheistic, but the nonviolence remains an almost inviolable constant. (Kraybill 1993)

The point is not that all of us should become Amish. The point is that Amish children grow up in a totally nonviolent culture. Amish parents teach their children about alternatives to violence from the time they are toddlers. It is the way in which adults handle even small incidents, the patterns of their responses to children's aggressive behavior, that leads to their children developing a deep respect for life.

Principle Two: Respect for Life Is Inviolable

Students must learn to respect all human life. This basic belief in the dignity of each person must be taught from preschool through graduation.

Respecting life implies an acceptance of all that is involved in being human — to have emotions, to lose control, to desire revenge, to feel fear, to lack self-esteem, or to seek meaning in one's life. Unfortunately, American schools overwhelmingly ignore the affective lives of students. Despite decades of reform — especially in middle schools, where interdisciplinary teams, block schedules, and longer homerooms attempt to meet some of the affective needs of students — schools still reflect a factory-model, assembly-line approach to emotional intelligence. Little could be more ineffective in building a culture in which whole-ness, emotional dimensions, the life of the spirit, the love of the arts, or any of many possible affective motivators could be employed to help students solve problems peacefully.

Student-centered, whole-child education integrates intellectual, social, and emotional development. These conditions must be met before a student can learn to respect his own life or the lives of others. And students must learn to respect life if they are to learn the skills of communication, negotiation, bridge-building, and compromise.

The role of the public school is to produce graduates who are decent people. But schools are not currently organized to accomplish that task. Thus teachers have the responsibility to incorporate the life of the emotions and spirit into various components of the curriculum and to be sensitive to their students' needs.

Principle Three: Build Community Cooperation

Working things out is a skill that can be taught, but it requires the commitment of the entire community. Families, communities, schools, and peer groups must work to educate every citizen in nonviolence and to pose the good of the group as equal in importance to preserving the rights of minority opinions.

While schools cannot be responsible for the conduct of the whole community, they can put the keys to a less violent world in each student's hands, which may then, in turn, affect the whole community. Schools must teach self-discipline, self-restraint, and self-esteem. Each day, educators must model the basic mediation skills that enable everyone either to agree or to cooperate despite their disagreements.

Conflict resolution is a way of life that must be worked at every day. Little will be gained when a school conducts a brief unit on violence prevention. Instead, the entire society in which children live must collaborate to produce a peaceful school community.

Principle Four: Adults Are Responsible for Youths' Safety

The protection offered to our children has been eroding. Some of the reasons are well known, such as the breakup of the family. Other factors include the ready availability of guns and drugs and the lack of hope for escaping poverty. Many children and youth become violent because they feel they have no other option. They live in virtual war zones, and their early lessons include diving to the ground when they hear gunfire.

If the society chooses not to shelter children but, instead, to expose them daily to life-threatening levels of violence, then it will have to cope with violent children. Children respond in kind. When they are protected, when someone responds to them if they feel danger, and when positive values are modeled regularly, children can unlearn aggression and acquire the beliefs that lead to peacemaking.

Principle Five: Honestly Assess Current Levels of Violence

It may seem simple to decide whether a particular school or school district has a problem with violence. However, there is a certain amount of subjectivity in interpreting data that can affect how school leaders view the problem. There usually are special interests that try to minimize the problems that may exist. Certain school officials will try to ignore the problem because of fears of losing their jobs, and some politicians will try to hide problems so they do not have to take the political risks necessary to solve them. School violence jeopardizes real estate prices, which involves other interests in defining the problem. Students, teachers, administrators, parents, businessmen, doctors, police, social workers,

41

and clergy all have diverse agendas for responding to or denying violent incidents in schools. These and many other factors will affect how problems are perceived. Communities are combinations of a wide variety of individuals with diverse agendas and multifaceted ways of thinking about what constitutes aggression in students and how to define school violence.

When a community admits it has a problem with school violence, then it must deal with that problem. But all real solutions have costs that communities often are unwilling to pay. Even such a superficial solution as requiring school uniforms will bring vocal protests from some groups, including students and parents. And more complex initiatives, such as block scheduling, include economic costs, as well as protests from community groups. Because effective antiviolence programs are multifaceted and systemic, they will include a large number of both economic and social costs. The arguments in the community can become particularly heated, which can pose very real threats to administrators' jobs.

Unfortunately, denying the problem of school violence will make it grow worse, until it can be almost impossible to solve. Kenneth Trump, president and CEO of National School Safety and Security Services in Cleveland, and J.B. Hylton of Hylton and Associates, Forensic Specialists, note that denial is a common feature of inadeqate safety plans in school districts. Excessive concern with creating a "pristine image" of the school leads to underreporting of incidents, ignoring the presence of gangs, and allowing illegal and violent activities to flourish (Hylton and Trump 1997).

When the first warning signs of a problem appear, schools need leaders who are willing to take the necessary risks to deal with that problem. Those leaders will need to put in an incredible number of frustrating hours talking to parents, negotiating with town leaders, responding to editorials and radio talk shows. Budgets will need to be increased for staff development and other costs. There will be protests from a variety of special interests with competing agendas.

If school leaders are to promote an honest discussion of school violence, they will need skill in handling the many social groups that must become involved. Local media must join the effort to report honestly every detail of the school crime occurring in their area. Administrators, local boards, the superintendent, and elected officials must join the Chamber of Commerce, the Tourist Bureau, local business owners, and even realtors to say, "Even though the data look worse now than when we denied the problem, it is now honest data. We now can begin to tackle this crisis and make it better."

Principle Six: Focus Less on Age and More on Effort

Unmotivated students often feel like prisoners in school. They gain greater satisfaction from trying to break out of this jail than from trying to be good inmates. Indeed, the public often shares these students' view; the image of compulsory school as a "holding tank" for children is common.

One school has helped to erase that image while, at the same time, reducing discipline problems. Chicago's DuSable High School is an intergenerational school in which students who dropped out at age 16 can come back to high school at 30 or 45 years of age (Toby 1993-1994). The intergenerational student body has provided serious models for younger students. Witnessing the desire to be educated among the older students, some younger students have chosen not to drop out, though they once had planned to do so. In addition, the adult attendance in the classes has made the inevitable problems with behavior easier for the teachers to handle.

It may not take an intergenerational school, such as DuSable, to bring many of the same benefits to troubled students. Just changing the age orientation used in most factory-type schools can signal to students that who they are and what they know are important. Thus continuous-progress schools or multiage environments can help students to progress without being labeled, consequently reducing alienation and the likelihood of school violence.

Principle Seven: Every Detail Counts

Cultivating a culture of nonviolence requires attention to the details. For example, recent research into lowered crime rates in

New York and other cities has indicated that arresting or citing such petty offenders as "squeegee men," those who urinate in public, panhandlers, etc., might have a dramatic effect on other crimes. The concept is called "tipping points" or "disorderliness"; and research suggests that where individuals feel they can get away with small infractions that create nuisance disorders (litter, petty theft, graffiti), they will inevitably try to commit larger crimes (Wilson 1985).

That principle is critical for schools. Orderliness, respect for persons and places, aesthetic considerations, and avoidance of all behaviors harmful to oneself or others are basic elements in maintaining community. The principal who picks up a candy wrapper in the hall is doing a lot more than usurping the janitor's role; the principal is stating that it is everyone's responsibility to keep the school spotless. When individuals are not permitted to smoke in the bathrooms, cut classes, curse, or engage in other small offenses, the authority of the school leaders and the school's sense of community grow. When nothing is done to curtail these behaviors, other offenses, even more criminal, often follow.

The psychology of disorder is rather straightforward: Crowded, unruly, and unsightly halls indicate lack of control and the probability of danger. Students then increase their hypervigilant behavior, looking for signs of trouble instead of assuming safe passage. Under these conditions, students are more likely to fear for their own safety than to commit to the good of the whole school. They feel no compunction to recognize the rules; they play at the fringes of what is allowed and do not respect the rationale behind the rules.

An orderly school also promotes respect for all forms of authority, including the teacher. Teachers inevitably demand respect and expect students to cooperate and perform. However, in disorderly environments this respect is absent and teachers even may be afraid to voice their expectations for students. Cohesive, relationship-centered, orderly, and attractive environments encourage students to discuss their frequent disengagement from school work and admit to petty infractions.

Principle Eight: Ready, Fire, Aim!

School communities dedicated to preventing violence need both to plan and to move instantly, to be both deliberate and spontaneous. This difficult task requires that planning take place on three levels: 1) short-term interventions designed to keep students safe and to stop dangerous behaviors; 2) the medium-range goals of learning how to follow processes that keep peace, such as resolving conflicts, handling peer mediations, and infusing respectful behavior into teacher behavior and the curriculum; and 3) the long-term goal of creating decent and responsible persons. Certainty is an illusionary goal. To be sure, there will be false starts, mistakes, and adjustments along the way. The aim will be modified frequently before the target is hit consistently.

It is easy to follow the above principles with students who are obedient, lovable, advantaged, and highly motivated. However, the measure of a school will be how well the adults follow these principles with students who do not appreciate their effort, who are disenfranchised, unmotivated, poor, and determined to be losers. Regardless of how well educators are treated by their students, they have the responsibility to model respect for all youth, to make school a place where democracy is the goal, and to ensure the safety of all children and youth who attend the school.

A peaceful school culture does not result by luck. It is the result of hard work. Violence is not inevitable in America's schools, but leaders must base their commitment to eradicate violence on a shared belief in the preciousness of all life. This will help educators to overcome their own denial while helping students learn to respect life and to cooperate.

References

Hylton, J.B., and Trump, K.S. *Hard Lessons in School Security.* Cleveland: National School Safety and Security Services, 1997.

Kraybill, Donald. Personal Communication, 5 June 1993.

National Center for Injury Prevention and Control. *The Prevention of Youth Violence: A Framework for Community Action*. Atlanta, Ga.: Centers for Disease Control and Prevention, 1993.

Richardson, V. "The Role of Attitudes and Beliefs in Learning to Teach." In *Handbook of Research on Teacher Education*, edited by John Sikula. New York: Macmillan, 1996.

Toby, Jackson. "Everyday School Violence: How Disorder Fuels It." *American Educator* 17 (Winter 1993-1994): 49, 44-48.

Wilson, James Q. *Thinking About Crime*. New York: Vintage, 1985.

Chapter Four

What Administrators Should Do

Administrators must stay alert to school safety concerns. While most administrators do pay attention to immediate school safety issues, they also need a long-term strategy, including a vision of what they want their schools to become, committees to plan and monitor programs, and a well-designed program to build students' peacemaking values and skills.

Of course, immediate safety concerns must be dealt with first. To meet these immediate needs, administrators should list the indicators of school safety. The checklist below is intended to increase awareness of some of the most visible indicators of school safety awareness. Eight or nine "yes" answers indicates a strong administrative awareness.

_____ 1. Do school staff patrol problem areas, such as hallways, stairwells, locker rooms, bathrooms, cafeterias, and school grounds?

_____ 2. Do school staff have regular, ongoing training in violence prevention and conflict resolution? Does the training include feedback from teachers, or is it limited to watching a video or listening to a speaker?

_____ 3. Are teachers evaluated according to how they handle violent students?

_____ 4. Does the school use security police, parents, off-duty police, substance-abuse monitors, or other volunteers as monitors to help staff patrol the school? Are the monitors trained to intervene in fights, to defuse violent situations, and to recognize drug users and sellers?

_____ 5. If buses or neighborhoods are not safe, are escorts available to ride on the buses and walk the children to their front doors?

_____ 6. What type of security is provided for teachers and students who stay after school?

_____ 7. Have weapons ever been sighted at the school? If so, is there an approved policy to deal with offenders?

_____ 8. How does the school know who should and who should not be present? Do visitors receive badges? How are new staff introduced? How long would it take to recognize a potentially dangerous stranger?

_____ 9. Does the school have some type of conflict resolution program? Is there a place where students can go to work out disagreements that may otherwise result in violence? Are counselors available and trained in conflict resolution? Do counselors have time to help students with other problems, such as gangs, suicide, or running away? Is there a peer-assistance program?

_____10. What are discipline guidelines designed to do? Do they provide both rewards for positive behavior and clear consequences for misbehavior?

_____11. Do teachers actually teach about the dangers of violence? Is violence prevention part of a number of courses, such as media criticism, social studies, health, and literature? Are news stories discussed or ignored? Is there a whole-school effort to be safe and a focus on the reverence for life?

Effective administrators build a culture of nonviolence by keeping up to date on research, by networking constantly, by caring deeply, and by persevering. They build their actions on a specific, obtainable vision. Most important, they do not accept the anti-quated notion of leadership that suggests that a successful leader is one who simply controls the students and faculty.

In schools with an authoritarian hierarchy, each level of administrator wields whatever power is necessary to keep peace among those in her or his "control." In such an atmosphere, "zero tolerance" means that there are few or no opportunities for misbehavior and few chances for students to learn from mistakes. Such schools are neither building a vision of community nor maximizing learning, because so much student time, thought, and energy goes into trying to foil the rules or escape what appear to be nonsensical punishments.

Authoritarian schools can provide short-term safety, assuming the punishments are severe enough to cause fear among the students. However, in the long run, such an approach yields, at best, only a record of "no incidents," rather than learning, community, and the fostering of decent adults. Instead, it results in a school that is more like a "holding tank" and an administrative style that is a form of despotic crowd control.

While the authoritarian administrative style is unlikely to lead to a truly nonviolent school, the "administrator as manager" style that became popular in the 1970s and 1980s can be dangerous. Merely delegating authority to teachers leaves the school without a central vision.

Instead, leaders for nonviolent schools must be models of the culture they wish to develop. They must substitute communication and relationship development for behaviors that seek merely to keep individuals "in line." They must understand and not further victimize youth who respond violently to a violent culture. At the same time, they must demonstrate the certain, swift, and logical consequences of violent behavior.

Researchers have studied successful principals in schools where students are poor, at-risk, and exposed daily to violence. Not only do these successful principals have certain beliefs in common, they also translate their beliefs into action and communicate these beliefs to teachers, parents, and the community at large. In particular, these successful principals:

1. Demonstrate leadership.
2. Create a visible commitment to learning.
3. Turn theory into practice and back to theory again.
4. Understand the role of the school for at-risk students.
5. Lead curricular and instructional change.
6. Create a positive school climate.
7. Evaluate schoolwide and personal success.
8. Make clear decisions.
9. Admit fallibility.
10. Build parent and community relations.
11. Take responsibility for student safety (Haberman 1996).

Demonstrate Leadership

The leader's decisions must be based on strongly held beliefs. To engender a culture of nonviolence, these beliefs must include a commitment to a safe environment conducive to learning and high expectations for faculty and students. By basing their decisions on their beliefs, these leaders turn the daily routines of school — taking attendance, making announcements, chairing committees, etc. — into meaningful events.

This ability to make meaning is vital for establishing a culture of nonviolence. Such meaning fills the vacuum many youth face when considering joining a gang or trying to resist drugs. In the absence of positive meaning created by the school's leaders, the students and faculty will create their own meanings, which may be very negative. For many poor youths in violent neighborhoods, meaning can be found in harmful rituals and negative activities, such as selling drugs, joining gangs, or using weapons. Meanings created out of danger, however frightening, are better than no meaning at all.

Making meaning requires more than just carrying out purely symbolic actions. The school leader must be invested in the school. That investment will be obvious in the way the leader communicates with faculty and students. The successful administrator pays attention to others. He or she also points out faculty strengths and expresses appreciation in a variety of ways for jobs well done. Most important, the successful administrator participates in those activities he or she has identified as priorities for others.

Teachers and students learn quickly whether an administrator is invested in the school. And the administrator's investment will yield a fund of moral authority and loyalty. That, in turn, will influence the faculty and students to "buy into" the leader's vision.

Administrators should design the school's discipline policies in order to help students learn the consequences of their actions, not just to punish them. Violent behavior of any type requires immediate intervention, and protecting students and teachers is the first priority. However, the success of the discipline policy will be based on whether students and teachers understand and agree with the concept behind the policy.

Offenses should be categorized so that the nature of an offense determines the type of intervention. One way is to separate offenses into three categories: 1) legal offenses, 2) institutional offenses, and 3) personal offenses. With this categorization, the type of intervention quickly becomes apparent.

In the first category of offenses, the administrator generally has little choice in responding. Such offenses as carrying a weapon, selling drugs, and theft are criminal activities. In these cases, administrators must report the illegal activity to the authorities.

For offenses that are institutional or personal, the administrator has more choices for an intervention. The key to effective interventions in these cases is clear, consistent communication. First, school leaders must communicate that the institution simply will not tolerate bullying, intimidation, extortion, cheating, and other aggressive behaviors. When administrators or teachers observe these behaviors, they must take quick and decisive measures. The violators, having made poor choices, must be made to discuss the consequences and must sign behavior contracts to stop the behavior immediately. In this way, the offender does not receive praise from his or her peers and thus is not rewarded for antisocial behavior.

At the third level, personal offenses, the violator is required to have serious talks with the administrator, counselor, or teacher.

These talks can be combined with group sessions and persuasive media designed to build empathy and interpersonal trust and to persuade the student to avoid behaviors that may violate institutional guidelines. This level of intervention is clearly the most powerful because it can prevent students from sliding into more serious offenses.

Create a Visible Commitment to Learning

The principal must make the commitment that nothing — not textbooks, bell schedules, tight budgets, or even state department of education rules — will get in the way of learning. The principal must resist the bureaucracy and its seemingly endless demands for paperwork when those demands interfere with the principal being visible and accessible in the school.

Such a commitment is especially challenging in neighborhoods where violence is frequent. But learning requires taking some risks. The effective principal will take students on field trips, bring in inspiring speakers, and focus on student effort more than on standardized tests. The goal is to do whatever one can to prevent irrelevance, disillusionment, and the deterioration of resilience among students and staff (Caine and Caine 1997).

Turn Theory into Practice and Back into Theory

Effective administrators put theories into practice and theorize about practices currently in use. They reflect on what motivates or disengages students and teachers, and they devise scenarios to address motivational needs.

In order to develop a nonviolent school, the principal must apply the research on what makes a school into a community of learners. The nature of how time is spent in school, the role of student assessment, and the definition of accountability may all change. The school must engage the students and treat them as part of a community, rather than as products to be processed. If not, then the students are more likely to react negatively to the school.

52

Understand the Role of the School for At-Risk Students

Researchers know quite a bit about how to help students succeed despite formidable hurdles ("resilient students"). It is common knowledge that mentoring, prosocial youth groups, sports, caring relatives, and religious organizations are important for resilience. If properly led, schools also can make a difference. But schools will not make that difference if the principal does not believe the school can play a pivotal role in the life of a poor, abused, neglected, violent, or drifting child.

The principal must play key roles in mobilizing neighborhood resources to add support to the lives of the neediest students. He or she will encourage teachers to find tasks that build competence and self-confidence in even the most reluctant learner. The key is to provide at-risk students with frequent, positive interactions with responsible adults. With a caring principal, a school can become the best chance a student has to see life in new, less violent terms.

Lead Curricular and Instructional Change

The negotiations that a principal must undertake in order to lead curricular change can themselves be a lesson to both students and teachers. As most administrators know, the numerous demands from state departments of education, special interests, parents, and other groups will contradict one another with irritating regularity. In the ensuing conversation, the community's priorities and strengths will be a lesson for teachers and students alike.

The principal must support a curriculum in which conflict resolution skills are both taught and practiced daily. That requires a larger vision of a peaceful community in which the leader models democratic behavior, values teacher-led initiatives to build community among students, and hires individuals who share a commitment to this vision.

Create a Positive School Climate

Creating meaning and building consensus require more of administrators than just naming site-based teams or revising policies.

They must change the culture of the school in order to overcome teachers' sense of isolation, lack of autonomy, and feelings of powerlessness. Administrators also must prevent burning out themselves. Conducting research, networking with other administrators, and observing other schools that successfully have reduced conflict will help administrators keep their vision alive.

Evaluate Schoolwide and Personal Success

It often is difficult to assess the work of a principal or other administrator. Motivating teachers for change, helping others to share a vision, and similar activities do not lend themselves to traditional evaluations. However, administrators must be able to evaluate their own work in order to make the constant adjustments that will be necessary to bring about lasting change in a school's culture.

One method for evaluating the administrator's work is to just count the number of violent incidents and check whether they are increasing or decreasing. However, it is more important in the long run for deeper, more subtle changes to occur in the culture of the school. When both students and teachers begin to use conflict resolution and other nonviolent techniques without constant reminders from administrators, then administrators will know that their efforts have succeeded.

Make Clear Decisions

Administrators not only must decide on the mission and goals of their schools, they also must decide how to get there. In order to communicate these decisions, administrators must understand the school's culture. This understanding determines how the administrator will talk about peace and conflict resolution, why students should resist drugs and gangs, and other topics.

There are certain assumptions administrators must make if they are to make effective decisions. For example, they must assume that individuals can be trusted, that information usually can be shared freely, and that everyone in the school has strengths upon which to base new learning. When administrators adopt these assumptions and clearly communicate their decisions, they will increase their chances to enjoy sustained levels of community support in the often-controversial arena of school safety and violence prevention (Lashway 1997).

Admit Fallibility

No one is infallible. If the school leader has built community support for a gang- or drug-resistance program and then discovers that the program is ineffective or, worse, inadvertently encourages gang membership or drug use, the leader must admit that he or she made a mistake.

Not all mistakes are created equal. Perhaps the worst mistake is to claim infallibility, to insist that one did not make a mistake. Insisting on infallibility fractures any moral authority a leader may have. On the other hand, free admission of mistakes, particularly those which can break trust, divide a community, or increase adversarialism, builds the leader's fund of moral authority. The leader's acknowledgment of the human capacity to err makes the important distinction between making a mistake and "being wrong," a lesson that everyone should learn.

Build Parent and Community Relations

Building a safe, nonviolent school requires a commitment to community relations that goes far beyond an annual parents' night. Strong home-school relationships result in higher student achievement, greater levels of safety and awareness, and fiscal and volunteer support. However, it takes excellent communication skills to marshal this support.

Some parents may fear the school learning too much about potential hazards to students in their homes. That is especially true for parents who have histories of arrests, who are substance abusers, or who possess weapons themselves. Administrators can overcome this wariness by making home visits, greeting the parents by name when they meet them, and encouraging them to volunteer for school tasks at which they can quickly succeed. Good communication skills, along with careful interpersonal skills, allow administrators to make even the poorest and most reluctant of parents indispensable allies in creating a safe school.

Take Responsibility for Student Safety

Administrators must take responsibility for school-related violence, whether within the school building or in the surrounding neighborhood. Student safety is the administrator's concern. However, the administrator must balance safety awareness with school climate issues. For example, if access to the school is limited to one door, that door may need to be more welcoming. If metal detectors are a routine part of school entry, additional efforts can be made to make the school look more inviting and less institutional.

Part of taking responsibility for student safety is to provide high-quality, ongoing staff development in violence prevention for all school staff. Such formal training should include anger management and conflict resolution for the staff themselves, because little is more damaging to a student antiviolence program than to tolerate teachers who are explosive or who manage their classes through external manipulation and control techniques.

Each principal should conduct an assessment of conditions in his or her school to identify safety concerns. The following checklist can be used to establish a school's "safety quotient" (Kadel and Follman 1993).

_____ 1. Main office: The main office should be easily found from all points in the complex.

_____ 2. Indoor lighting: All areas accessible to students and staff — including stairwells, hallways, and closets — should be well-lit during times of operation. Areas not used and not lit should be inaccessible to students. For example, many crimes occur under stairwells; and administrators must find ways to eliminate access to such areas. Hall monitors should be able to see all areas easily.

_____ 3. Outside lighting: The building should be either totally lit or totally dark at night. Experiments with keeping a building totally dark and having watchful neighbors report any lights to the police have proven effective. Either way, lighting should be designed for safety more than for aesthetic or financial concerns.

_____ 4. Fences: Some construction and fencing strategies may result in a school looking more like a prison. One way to maintain an inviting appearance is by wisely choosing the security fences. Many experts now recommend using wrought-iron instead of chain-link fences. Chain-link fences can be climbed or cut. Wrought-iron fences are difficult to climb or cut and are easily padlocked. They also are more attractive.

_____ 5. Greenery: Shrubs add greatly to the appearance of a school. Trees and bushes should be planted at least 10 feet from the school walls and should be kept small and well-trimmed, exposing the ground. Ensure that trees do not provide a way to the roof.

_____ 6. Architecture and equipment: Avoid decorative ledges and ensure that drain pipes cannot be scaled. Keep dumpsters and other equipment away from the sides of buildings so they cannot be used as access to the roof.

_____ 7. Doors: The trend is to lock all the doors except the main entrance and to monitor access. Back doors, where activity tends to be less frequent or where unidentified delivery personnel may make it more difficult to tell who does and does not belong, should be especially secure. The windows in classroom doors should not be covered by posters, because that can increase teacher isolation and danger or may prevent individuals in the hall from observing a hostage situation.

_____ 8. Windows: Windows may be used as access for guns, drugs, or other illicit substances, as well as intruders. However, windows also can be used as a safe route for evacuation. Windows can be designed so that smuggling can be prevented while still providing emergency exits, when necessary.

_____ 9. Bathrooms: Faculty and staff visits to student bathrooms may curb graffiti, smoking, and other acts of aggression.

_____ 10. Lockers: All lockers should be easily visible. Lockers in corners, alcoves, or extremely crowded areas are difficult to supervise and may harbor intruders or may be easy places to hide illegal substances or weapons.

_____ 11. Parking lots: Parking lots for students and staff should be well-monitored. Some experts suggest mixing faculty and student parking for further security. Also, the lots and drives should be designed to discourage through traffic and speeding, and rocks and loose gravel should be kept off of lots and roadways.

_____ 12. Security systems: The school's fire and police alarms should be in good working order and checked regularly. Closed-circuit television monitors can be used to help security personnel patrol the building, and telephones and intercoms can help teachers and administrators communicate during an emergency. In addition, such low-tech systems as formal identification cards and stickers for visitors can help faculty and staff quickly identify anyone who does not belong in the building.

_____ 13. Talk to students: Students know best where they feel afraid and why. Administrators also might consider using a telephone answering machine or even an old-fashioned suggestion box that students can use to provide anonymous tips about impending student criminal behavior.

When auditing building safety, it is important to make visual inspections, take surveys, and talk to students, teachers, and parents. The principal should note those changes that need to be made immediately, such as locks, signs, or fencing.

While incidents may occur in even the most carefully laid out environments and under the most scrupulous plans, administrators who focus their attention on high-risk student populations and hazardous areas will lower the likelihood of violence and reap maximum returns for their efforts.

The School Safety Plan

Every school should have a school safety plan, including a school safety committee and a crisis management team.

The school safety plan is the overall framework used to keep students safe, to foster conflict resolution skills, and to build resistance to any threat of violence. The school safety plan constitutes the first, most general, and most visionary level of peace-building activity; it is a framework for action. In the plan, school leaders spell out, in simple language, the attitudes and behaviors they desire, the approaches to foster these attitudes and behaviors, and the programs to meet goals. It should cover all areas of school climate, disciplinary policy, attendance, safety, and security. School safety plans usually are established for entire districts.

There should be a school safety committee at both the district and building levels. The building-level committees implement initiatives at each site, oversee building-level safety concerns, and provide feedback to the district committee. Building-level committees must have the authority to hear about safety concerns from all teachers, parents, and community members and must be able to address them expeditiously. They should be a proactive group empowered to consider a vast number of options to stop violence before it starts. Members of these school safety committees should represent a wide variety of constituencies: parents, students, medical personnel, psychologists, social workers, police, youth workers, and school administrators.

The school safety committee produces a plan that includes short-term, interim, and long-term violence prevention strategies. Short-term strategies are designed to eliminate the immediate dangers to students. These strategies include conducting a security assessment and establishing the crisis management team. Interim strategies are the programs that become part of the student learning process, such as training students to be peer mediators. Finally, the long-term strategies produce students who are responsible citizens of a democratic nation.

The crisis management team, as its name suggests, is the front line of defense in times of emergency. Its members should include a school psychologist, counselor, nurse, local rabbi or priest, crossing guard, etc., who will be in important positions during a crisis. The members of the crisis management team may also be part of the school safety committee.

The members of both the school safety committee and the crisis management team should receive frequent, high-quality training. A group of concerned individuals, however well-educated and articulate, is not necessarily well informed about the nature of community violence, gang indicators and characteristics, weapons, the role of alcohol in violent behavior, or other topics that will be relevant to their work. Administrators also will need to mobilize community resources to address specific concerns. For example, if sexual harassment is a problem in a middle school, the president of the local rape prevention council might conduct seminars for teachers or work with individual students or parents. Other local resource people who will be useful to the committees include police, social workers, university experts, or others experienced in conflict resolution, alcohol abuse prevention, gang suppression, etc.

The crisis management team develops specific plans for responding to crises, including designating the individuals who will perform specific roles in an emergency. The plan also should include a series of code phrases that allow the staff to be alerted to crises without alarming the students. All individuals in the building should hold practice crisis alert procedures at least yearly.

The crisis management plan should be very specific. It should specify who does what task and how they do it. It should identify who will be in charge if the principal is not in the building, who will answer the telephones, and even who will identify wounded or dead students for the police.

In addition, every staff member in the school should be given copies of the plans for specific emergencies. For example, anyone who is likely to receive a telephone call should have a Bomb Threat Report Form. That form will include the following questions:

1. When is the bomb expected to explode?
2. Where is the bomb located right now?

3. What does it look like?

4. Who are you and why did you plant the bomb?

Staff members should be trained to keep asking these questions in order to get as much information as possible from a caller, even though callers usually will not answer most of the questions (NSSC 1990).

Officials in Cypress-Fairbanks School District in northwest Harris County, TX., were undoubtedly thankful they had their crisis management plan operable on 14 November 1992 when a domestic dispute between the school's educational diagnostician and her estranged husband erupted into violence. The husband entered the school grounds, chased his ex-wife across the campus, shot her fatally, then shot himself. Fortunately, few if any of the students were aware of the emergency when a coded announcement indicated to teachers that all doors were to be locked and students kept inside until further notice. About a half-hour after the slayings took place, students were released through other doors. Many students had no idea what had taken place until they heard it on the news later that evening. When school resumed the following Monday, psychologists were available to help students sort out their feelings (Bardwell 1992).

During a crisis, communication is imperative. Ready means of communication should include connections between classrooms, labs, the nurse, the main office, and the school grounds. Cell phones can be used on playgrounds and in hallways, and every classroom should have a telephone or intercom. It is ironic that many classrooms are wired for the Internet yet remain without a telephone or intercom to call the main office. Administrators must include this equipment in the site budget.

References

Bardwell, S.K. "Domestic Dispute Turns Fatal at Cy-Fair School." *Houston Post*, 14 November 1992, p. 92.

Caine, R., and Caine, G. *Education on the Edge of Possibility*. Alexandria, Va.: Association for Supervision and Curriculum Development, 1997.

Haberman, M. "The Star Administrator Selection Interview." Brochure. Houston: Haberman Educational Foundation, 1996.

Kadel, S., and Follman, J. *Reducing School Violence*. Tallahassee: Florida Department of Education, March 1993.

Lashway, L. "Visionary Leadership." *ERIC Digest* (January 1997). http://www.ed.ed.gov/databases/ERIC_Digests/ed402643.html.

National School Safety Center (NSSC). *School Crisis and Prevention*. Malibu, Calif.: Pepperdine University, March 1990.

Chapter Five

What Teachers Should Do

Teachers must build a humane community within each classroom. Such a classroom can alleviate the conditions that cause many children to turn to gangs and violence. A humane classroom allows students to develop self-respect. It provides them with role models for solving problems in nonviolent ways. And it gives them hope for the future.

In order to create a humane classroom and school, teachers first must work with each other. Perhaps the first task of a school's teachers is to reach a consensus on their goals and to articulate their shared convictions about the importance of nonviolence. Once that has been done, the hard work of choosing particular programs and strategies becomes much easier. When teachers share beliefs, they find it easier to debate such often contentious issues as punishment vs. consequences, bribes vs. intrinsic rewards, and coercion vs. correction. Thus more energy can be spent on reaching their goals.

Teachers also must become skilled in using violence prevention strategies. Thus they should demand ongoing, high-quality staff development. Schools regularly should provide instruction for teachers and staff in how to handle potentially violent classroom interactions; and the information provided should be age, population, and culture specific. And the staff development should involve custodians and other support staff in addition to teachers and administrators.

Perhaps most important, teachers should build trust with their students. To do that, they must learn not to fear their students while also understanding the role that peer pressure plays in their students' behavior.

When teachers fear their students, they often "clamp down" and use "zero tolerance" policies to prevent student violence (Dill and Stafford 1996). This reflexive reaction to fear will backfire, because these teachers will reduce the amount of student-teacher interaction that occurs in class. If teachers are afraid to be alone with a student after class, they cannot have the one-on-one conversations with students that provide them with the access to adults that they need to combat peer pressure. In addition, the students will rebel against the teacher's repressive efforts. When teachers avoid controlling students through coercion or repression, they teach the students to control themselves.

How teachers manage their own stress helps students to develop ways to get along and succeed. Acting arbitrarily and overpowering students, instead of cooperating to find agreement, legitimizes the students' own inclinations to overpower one another. In contrast, creating a humane and democratic classroom in which students learn the reasons for decisions nurtures in them a legitimate sense of self-control.

Teachers must keep constantly in mind the effects that peer pressure will have on student reactions. It does not matter whether the teacher is asking for legitimate behavior from a student. If the student believes that his or her classmates will perceive the teacher's request as disrespectful, the student will react negatively.

The teacher must avoid even the subtlest of "put-downs," even when correcting a student. Consider this example:

Teacher: Theresa, did you bring that book you had out? It's overdue.
Theresa: No, Miss. I forgot it.

> Teacher (in front of class): Well, am I going to have to call your Mother?
>
> Theresa: Call my mother, Bitch! I don't give a damn!

Here is another way the same encounter could have gone.

> Teacher: Theresa, did you bring that book you had out? It's overdue.
>
> Theresa: No, Miss. I forgot it.
>
> Teacher: Okay, let's talk before you leave class today.
>
> Theresa: Okay, Miss.

In the first example, Theresa believed that she had been humiliated in front of her peers. While the teacher did not intend to challenge Theresa's self-respect, Theresa cannot afford to let a display of condescension or authority from the teacher go unanswered in front of her friends. Thus she must respond to the teacher with an insult and swearing in order for her peers to continue to think of her as "cool."

In the second example, the opportunity for peers to witness the teacher challenging Theresa was cut off by the teacher's decision to have a private conversation about the book. That also prevented Theresa from displaying arrogance in front of her friends. The teacher still can tell Theresa that she is going to confront her parent. However, no one else has to know that.

Conversations in school differ dramatically from those outside of school, reflecting the reality that students and teachers have relationships on a wide variety of levels. Behavior between students and teachers when peers are watching is sure to differ greatly from behavior that occurs between a student and teacher when peers are absent.

The quality of the private conversations that a student and teacher have will give the student an idea of how much this teacher is willing to invest in him or her. A student may not acknowledge that a teacher really cares, but this knowledge will not be lost on the student. It will make a difference in his or her life.

However, it is a mistake to assume that a positive conversational relationship between a student and teacher will override peer relationships in the classroom. That rarely happens. A teacher who has established an easy conversational relationship with a student should not be surprised or upset when that student acts out in class. Teachers must remember that, at all times, peer approval vies with every other dynamic in a student's life. Forced into a choice, students almost always will side with their peers against the teacher, no matter how much the student likes the teacher.

Researchers have observed specific actions that characterize teachers who succeed with students who are poor, at-risk, or violent (Haberman 1996). Such teachers are not judgmental. Their first inclination is to understand and communicate, not to characterize or condemn. They are not moralistic, knowing keenly the difference between preaching and teaching. Successful teachers of students in violent schools are not easily shocked. Rather than focus on their own feelings about how traumatizing or horrific an event might be, these teachers ask first, "Where can I get help for this child?" If they can help, they do; if a professional can provide better help, these teachers refer the student to that professional. If no one can be of help, they get on with their lives and their teaching.

Teach Individuals, Not Classes

Curricular frameworks and textbooks can disempower students because students may lack cultural familiarity with these materials. Unlike textbook-based approaches, student-centered learning validates the student's current experience by focusing on the familiar and moving toward the unfamiliar.

A "constructivist" form of teaching defines the student's world as a source of valuable information and insight. It allows students to use what they already know to gain a greater sense of control and mastery. While constructivist teaching is more difficult than teaching from the textbook or worksheets, it is a genuine education that will produce citizens aware of and capable of abiding by the law, working honestly at a job, and building a democracy.

Pay Attention to Routines

Many at-risk students do not know how to schedule their day so that, for example, they can reach school at eight o'clock. No one has taught them how to determine how much time it will take to get ready in the morning. Poor children may not wake at the same time every day, may not be routinely bathed, and may not eat regularly. For many of these children, chaos is the norm. For this reason, predictability, structure, and routine are critical.

Children enjoy analyzing time and can be taught to judge when they will arrive someplace, which events took too much time in order to meet the schedule, and whether they could have slept a few minutes longer. This is a vital skill for both school and life.

For the same reasons, at-risk children need stable routines while in school. These routines include the organization of the school day, as well as routines for each lesson. These routines provide the students with predictability and order, which can be sorely lacking in other aspects of their lives.

Provide Opportunities for Failure

While it is important that many classroom experiences enable success, that success may come, for growing minds, only after a considerable number of attempts. Students need to see the value of making mistakes, analyzing them, and trying again. In that way, they learn the value of staying with a goal, persisting, and not becoming a victim.

Avoid Labels

"Oh, you have Lorenzo and Jeremy! How will you make it through the year?" That is not an uncommon comment in teachers' lounges across the country. However, it is the hallmark of a disrespectful school.

It is too easy to label a student. Teachers often make assumptions about a child because the child has a parent in trouble with the law or because the child lives in a certain complex or block. And teachers' views have a way of becoming self-fulfilling prophecies, passed from teacher to teacher so that the child never has a chance to escape the label. Being labeled and caricatured can only increase a student's loss of hope, feelings of victimization, and alienation from prosocial efforts.

Students from violent environments or who are prone to violence almost always can be "referred away." Each of them, if scrutinized closely enough and long enough, can be diagnosed with something. But teachers seeking to create a culture of nonviolence usually do not refer their students for testing or special education; rather, they try to keep them in the classroom community, avoid labeling, and model humane approaches to teaching them.

Respond Appropriately to Offenses

Teachers must be able to identify quickly the kind of offense a student has committed and then to choose the appropriate response. The categories used for identifying offenses should be ones on which the entire faculty and administration has agreed; students need consistency from class to class. For example, the school might agree on the following categorization of offenses: 1) illegal acts, 2) offenses against school rules, and 3) personal offenses.

Some offenses may fall into all three categories. The guiding principle in these cases is that the offense is dealt with at its highest level. For example, a youth who carries an illegal knife or gun onto a campus and shows it in class is offending at all three levels; but because that offense is an illegal act, it should be dealt with at that level. On the other hand, a youth who refuses to join small-group activities or who calls out constantly in class is committing offenses best dealt with first at the personal level.

All three levels of intervention function simultaneously in the school, communicating to students that adults in the school will not tolerate lack of cooperation, aggression, or any behaviors that affect the quality of learning in the school.

In many cases, a nonpunitive discussion of the ramifications of daily behavior problems can avoid the need for punishments. These discussions should center on concrete examples that children can understand, for example, how the misbehavior of some students can make them all late for recess. By discussing consequences and expecting students to be accountable, teachers can build in their classrooms a community in which trust will be a dynamic force for learning as well as societal change.

Students need to understand that consequences are a logical and inexorable result of behaviors. The focus on consequences that is available in a well-structured classroom makes it possible for teachers to point to differences and the impact these differences have.

Persist

Creating a humane and democratic classroom requires incredible persistence, especially when the students are accustomed to authoritarian models. These students will resist real learning and will favor rote activities. The effort in making their own decisions can be frustrating to youths, and those with hair-trigger tempers may unexpectedly become violent.

Many students, when first experiencing a democratic classroom, will be unsure and will consciously or subconsciously sabotage the whole process in favor of teacher behaviors with which they are more familiar. They may act out, verbally accost students who are participating, or simply refuse to participate themselves. What they are awaiting is the teacher's words signaling acquiescence to the lowest academic common denominator: "Okay. I see you can't handle this. Open your books to page 13 and do the odd-numbered problems."

When faced with this student reaction, the teacher must not give up. The skills learned in a democratic classroom — solving problems, predicting, planning, and guessing consequences — are vital for children learning to escape the culture of violence. Students will develop risk-taking and problem-solving skills slowly, so the teacher must model these skills by talking to themselves out loud, thus demonstrating the thought processes involved (Dill and Stafford 1996).

Guidelines for Elementary Teachers

In elementary schools, formal student instruction should include courses in anger management, conflict resolution, and peer mediation. They should rely on demonstration and real-life examples and should include plenty of practice sessions. The lessons from these courses also should be integrated into other courses, such as civics, language arts, social studies, and art.

Teachers should frequently articulate the basic lessons from these courses. Some of the children may never have heard these assumptions at home; indeed, some children will come from homes that support or encourage violence. In particular, even the youngest children should learn that:

1. It's okay to make mistakes; mistakes help us learn how to change our behavior.
2. It's okay to need help with problems.
3. Most people avoid violence, do not carry weapons, and succeed in working things out with words.
4. Glamorizing brutality, aggression, or coercion is wrong; the media can mislead us.
5. Not all sources of information are helpful. Gangbangers, neighborhood thugs, and even relatives and friends can tell you something that turns out to be dangerous.
6. Asking questions is smart.
7. While adults want to help and protect children, children themselves must be partners in violence prevention.

Elementary schools should have a formal peer-mediation training program for older students. There are a variety of programs available. When disputes break out, the peer mediators immediately approach the disputing students and offer to mediate. Teachers also can refer students to peer mediators. The peer mediators can wear special jerseys, caps, or vests to indicate their function.

Older elementary students can understand such basic words as *aggression, threat, compromise, resolve,* and *nonviolent*; and they can list concrete reasons why violent resolutions to problems are inappropriate. They can understand positive and negative models and be able to choose appropriate models in hypothetical situations. Among the learning activities that can be used with upper elementary students are:

- Perform a skit in which they say the words they might use to refuse joining in vandalism or violence.
- Describe how violence affects the mind and body and discuss consequences of violent behaviors
- Discuss how the media glamorize violence and acculturate children to think that hurting others is funny.
- List and discuss coping strategies they might use when they feel rejected, tempted, scared, or harassed.
- Discuss the reasons for valuing their own lives and the lives of others.

By the age of seven or eight, students can see the connection between the proactive curriculum and the consequences of inappropriate behavior. Each teacher who helps make these multiple connections for students, both in curricular and extracurricular contexts, will reinforce the desired values. When individual students need ongoing intervention for violent behavior, the school culture will support them.

Guidelines for Middle School Teachers

When students move from the small and personal environment of an elementary school to the larger, often anonymous atmosphere of a middle school, teachers need to reassert nonviolence as the only accepted norm. Individuals who behave inappropriately must be sanctioned using nonpunitive and rational consequences; they may not participate in the celebrations or benefits of the community at large until their behavior changes. They cannot be allowed to ruin events for others. In effect, teachers will define members of the community as those who are nonviolent and will categorize the violent students as outsiders. That is a powerful incentive for middle-schoolers, whose behavior is often driven by the need to belong.

Teachers also must become intimately acquainted with the middle-schoolers' apparently ephemeral and fluid culture. Middle-schoolers speak their own language, which may be even more difficult to understand if racial, ethnic, or other cultural dif-

71

ferences are numerous. Teachers culturally mismatched to students may not even know how little they are communicating. Yet skilled communication with students is vital to overcoming oppositional behavior and remaining a community. Just one trusting teacher can save a student from dangerous, self-wounding, or academically damaging behavior by establishing trust and building a relationship.

Students' communication skills should be emphasized throughout the whole curriculum. These skills will help bridge cultural divides and will make both students and teachers aware of stereotypes or prejudices they may have about one another. This focus on communication may include making speeches, journal writing, extemporaneous discussions in class, or "student court" arguments. Special attention should be paid to a student's ability to listen, since accurately hearing another's story is the foundation of the mediation process. Increased communication skills will contribute greatly to middle school students' abilities to negotiate differences and reach consensus.

Middle school students can master conflict resolution and negotiation skills if these are taught directly and experientially. If students are able to observe teachers using these skills on a daily basis, they will learn and adopt peacemaking skills at an even faster pace. Among the skills that even the most disruptive middle school students can learn are:

1. To think before they speak, even if greatly provoked. When a middle school student fails in this area, she or he should reflect on the role that thinking before speaking would have played in avoiding conflict.
2. To use conflict resolution and negotiating skills as they speak.
3. To encourage other students to resolve differences nonviolently; to apply positive peer pressure.
4. To articulate the benefits of collaboration and the disadvantages of adversarial approaches or competition.
5. To name the elements of conflict and to be able to identify escalating and de-escalating strategies.

6. To name and identify anger triggers, to correctly distinguish behaviors that increase anger from behaviors that de-escalate anger, and to increase measurably their own levels of tolerance.
7. To distinguish between "wrong" and "different." Middle school students build empathy for diverse opinions and practices by understanding that their perceptions of others may be biased, that knowledge builds understanding, and that conformity is not a moral value.

Guidelines for High School Teachers

Few high schools make much effort to center their programs on students' developmental needs, despite evidence that the needs of high school students are as great as those of middle-schoolers. Instead, most high schools focus on external control in order to deal with the large crowds of students; and the resulting anonymity makes most high schools precarious places for students in general and particularly precarious for students at risk. Under these conditions, high school teachers have even greater challenges in supporting the school's mission to nurture nonviolent and responsible youth.

High school students benefit from constant teacher attention to active listening, taking perspective, dealing with anger, learning to differentiate aggression from assertiveness, and learning to overcome bias. While these skills should be taught at a basic level in the middle school, they should be reinforced and expanded in the high school.

High school teachers should:

- Avoid keeping track of wrongs, even mentally, or of humiliating students whose behavior is substandard but not illegal.
- Demonstrate self-evaluation by talking aloud to students about the processes of making decisions. They should discuss successful and unsuccessful decisions they have made and the consequences of those decisions.
- Articulate their own vulnerability to prejudices, admit fallibility, and show how some mistakes are more serious than others.

- Support conflict resolution, peer mediation, and other service programs.
- Refer students to mediation, then follow up and encourage students who have used the service. Teachers should join in mediations when appropriate.

About 15 to 20 hours of training are necessary for teachers to learn how to mediate disputes at the high school level (NAME 1995). Training for teachers is imperative in order to secure their support, to demonstrate the school's advocacy of peacemaking as a top priority, and to ensure that all teachers understand the fundamentals of the school's mediation program. Building teacher support through adequate training and discussion is especially critical in the high school, where such specialties as physics, psychology, literature, etc., may build expertise in subjects at the expense of a vision for the whole institution.

Among the skills that high school students may be expected to master are:

- Anger management and walking-away skills. High school students also should be able to use the language of conflict resolution in halls, bathrooms, classrooms, or playing fields to prevent violence.
- Accurately predict, dramatize, discuss, or write about the natural consequences of institutional or illegal offenses.
- Demonstrate intrinsic motivation to do well in school, serve the community, and stay out of illegal activities. High school students have internalized some of the guidelines for getting along with diverse, even antagonistic others; they should realize it is their responsibility to tolerate behavior that is not ideal in order to maintain social order.
- Teach or co-teach conflict resolution lessons for peers or as leaders of teams that visit middle or elementary schools to discuss nonviolence.

High school students should participate in projects that serve those less fortunate than they are. Service projects help at-risk youth focus on what they have, not their deficits, and on what they can give, not what they wish to take from society. Service and the skills it brings build self-esteem and increase the students' respect for those they serve.

Summary

There are general skills that all teachers need if they are to foster a nonviolent culture. Regardless of the age of their students, successful teachers:

- Never employ shame or humiliation. They never publicly discuss private matters with students; and they never scream, scold, or harangue.
- Use students' interests to involve them in learning.
- Demonstrate empathy for students' expressions of feelings. They listen to students and respect them.
- Teach and model mediation skills. Successful teachers model cooperation with all other adults in the building.
- Never get caught in escalating punishments to force compliance. Successful teachers defuse, sidestep, and redirect challenges to their authority.
- Identify student pain, sickness, and abuse. Refer students to people who can help.
- Focus on effort and not on innate gifts or abilities. Successful teachers encourage student effort by finding good parts in their work.
- Use cooperative learning whenever appropriate.
- Do not try to control children by calling on them when they are not paying attention.
- Model learning from mistakes and differentiate this from expecting students to learn through repeated failures. Repeated failures lead to frustration, but learning from mistakes leads to success.
- Show respect for parents in the presence of their children (Haberman and Dill 1994).

References

Dill, V., and Stafford, D. "Push: Teaching the Children of Neglect." *Educational Forum* 61 (Fall 1996): 36-45.

Haberman, M. *Star Teachers of Children in Poverty*. West Lafayette, Ind.: Kappa Delta Pi, 1996.

Haberman, M., and Dill, V. "Can Teachers Be Educated to Save Students in a Violent Society?" In *Teachers as Leaders*, edited by Donovan R. Walling. Bloomington, Ind.: Phi Delta Kappa Educational Foundation, 1994.

National Association for Mediation in Education (NAME). *Standards for Peer Mediation Programs*. Washington, D.C.: National Institute for Dispute Resolution, 1995.

Chapter Six

The Role of
Support Services

Three characteristics describe support programs that work. First, successful support services neutralize attitudes of entitlement to violent behavior by providing for immediate relief from danger, pain, neglect, or abuse. Second, they promote growth, responsibility, and accountability and are not merely punitive. And third, support programs that reduce aggression and victimization do so by insisting that violent students take responsibility for their crimes and make amends whenever possible; that is, they provide genuine restitution.

There are two types of support services, those that prevent violence and those that intervene after an incident. Preventive programs include after-school sports or clubs, as well as those that offer training in conflict resolution and peer mediation or help youths to resist gangs and drugs. Preventive programs also include those designed to change the community's culture to encourage nonviolence.

Of the second type of support services, those that intervene after an incident, those that have the most positive effect on the long-term peacefulness of a school are the programs that require restitution from the perpetrator and compensation of the victims. A support program of this type should be available at every school.

It is important for these programs to distinguish between punishment and restitution. If a student who has harassed a girl is made to pick up the trash on the playground, that is only punishment and will have little long-term effect. Restitution requires that the offender take responsibility for the offense, for example, by apologizing, attending seminars on harassment, and helping to reduce harassment by others (Bazemore and Day 1996). In the same way, it makes little sense for a violent student to spend time in the principal's office unless it was the principal who was attacked.

Regardless of the particular designs of a program that intervenes after an incident, it is necessary to provide immediate relief when it is needed. This may mean removing a dangerous student from the school, supplying emergency counseling or medical treatment, or meeting other short-term needs.

There are a variety of organizations that provide support services for schools and communities. These include government agencies, volunteer service organizations, clubs, professional groups, private organizations, and the media. School administrators should be familiar with the organizations in their area, as well as with the major professional organizations in education. They also should be aware of such national organizations as the American Medical Association, the Association of Black Physicians, the NAACP, the Urban League, the Center to Prevent Handgun Violence, and Educators for Social Responsibility, which are prominent among groups working to reduce violence. A list of selected organizations is provided in the Resources section of this book.

For schools to work well with these agencies, educators must plan carefully. They need to make sure that the purposes of the support group also match specific, local goals. Even such details as where to hold meetings are important. Is the room large enough? Can the furniture be moved?

Educators also must keep the community informed about the available support services. The goal is to get the word out to as many people and from as many directions as possible. Therefore the school must sponsor meetings at various times. Many working parents find it easier to attend a meeting in the evening. Many parents also would need to arrange for child care.

Educators need to reach as many community members as possible. Thus meetings need to be held in a variety of settings, not only schools but also local houses of worship, neighborhood watch groups, business groups, and others. This multiple-settings approach increases the number of voices speaking about the program, which speeds the rate at which a whole community becomes excited about the subject.

When schools institute programs that can change the status quo and that require collaboration with other community groups, there usually are three stages that precede the initial successes of those programs. In the first stage, the general denial that there is a problem is overcome. The schools and the support agencies begin organizing, and school boards make policy. In the second stage, various groups cooperate and set mutual goals. However, the problems that the programs were designed to address may just move somewhere else in the community, causing conflict in the community. In the third stage, there likely will be charges of ineffective programs, institutional racism, and corruption.

If the educators and community members who support these programs understand that those three stages are likely to occur before the programs demonstrate results, they will be less likely to get discouraged, quit, or try a quick, political fix to a complex problem. In the course of learning how to collaborate with a variety of constituencies, certain individuals with moral leadership will emerge. Ideally, the needs of youth will inspire local groups to do whatever it takes to create workable, comprehensive programming (OJJDP 1994).

When community organizations and schools combine, they can reinforce efforts to help youth resist what is often a taxing, even toxic, culture in which to grow. These partnerships are even more successful when they include a great deal of parent involvement.

A variety of community programs have proven successful. Some of them are described below.

Student Assistance Programs (SAPs)

Student assistance programs (SAPs) involve the efforts of a team of specialists to both prevent and solve youth problems. Services are designed to keep children healthy and to prevent them from falling prey to any number of physical or cultural predators. SAPs provide the help needed in a way that suits the child or family, not in a way that meets the needs of the service provider. Remboldt explains:

> Student assistance programs coordinate an already established continuum of services ideally organized and focused on addressing each element of a systemic problem . . . including preventive education for students, teachers, and community leaders; identification of problems; intervention with troubled students; referral of student to appropriate resources; support groups providing graduated levels of support for different target groups of students; parent education and training, and community support. (1994, p. 38)

SAP teams may include school psychologists, administrators, counselors, teachers, parents, police officers, probation officers, child welfare workers, district attorneys, housing authority representatives, security officers, or custodians. Efficient student assistance programs knit together all available resources to focus on individual student needs.

Student assistance programs vary widely in their focus. In many cases, school social workers coordinate with case workers to provide whatever services students need. Students may be referred to programs designed to help them resist drugs or peer pressure or to teach them life skills. Student assistance programs may be combined with conflict resolution, peer mediation, and support groups. In such instances, promising youth may be identified to receive intensive training, which not only benefits them but also may change their beliefs in order to reduce their feelings of entitlement to violent reactions. High success rates with at-risk students are reported regularly when the student assistance programs are

80

supported by concerted adult action, involvement, commitment, and follow-through (Remboldt 1994).

Some student assistance programs also address the medical needs of at-risk students. Violent students often emerge from highly vulnerable, poor, and dysfunctional families. Their first contact with the medical system usually is in the emergency room of a hospital. Emergency physicians may wish to communicate directly with schools and social services regarding these students and their families. They often use only the emergency room because they lack insurance.

Inoculations, glasses or hearing aids, prenatal health care, nutrition information, or psychological testing for learning disabilities may vastly improve the lives of poor students and increase their capacity to learn and stay in school. The school-linked medical services of student assistance programs also can be the point of entry for some family members to receive counseling, enter therapy, or begin to overcome addictions (Hechinger 1992).

Effective student assistance programs remain flexible, meeting a variety of student needs. Seldom does a student become violent due to only one risk factor; a multiplicity of factors interact. Some programs may work for some youth but not for others. Therefore social workers or teachers working in student assistance programs use many different types and levels of services simultaneously: health organizations, professional organizations, religious groups, or others, whatever approach is best suited for the student. For this reason, single-purpose student assistance programs are less likely to prevent violence than are those with a full menu of services.

In addition, considerable research supports making all th vices available at one location (Lane, Richardson, and VanBe 1996). Unfortunately, these on-site support programs are s the minority.

Community School Policing Programs

The role and make-up of local community school policin; grams have different characteristics in different schools. '

81

programs generally require coordination among social workers, counselors, and juvenile justice professionals. Increasingly, these teams include fully trained police. Often called "school liaison officers" or "resource police," fully trained officers become integral players in the school's violence prevention program when departments follow well-researched methods of community policing.

Full-time school liaison officers usually are assigned to comprehensive middle or high schools. They make arrests for tobacco and substance abuse, assaults, and other misdemeanors; and generally they emphasize the message that what is illegal outside of school will not be tolerated inside school. However, their prevention activities are equally important. These police may prevent students from carrying guns by increasing awareness of how school violence can escalate, how volatile and vulnerable individuals can be who carry weapons, and how drugs, alcohol, and guns often create a criminal mix. Students may tip the officers about upcoming parties that might become dangerous. Police working in schools and in neighborhoods around schools also have organized chapters of Students Against Drunk Driving, worked to prevent suicides, and built skateboard ramps so kids have something to do after school (Williams 1996).

The school liaison officers should be called on frequently to present programs or conduct informal interviews at the school. It is important for students to see police as their advocates, not just as adversaries when the students get in trouble. This enables students to be relaxed around police. Gang suppression units and other initiatives should be designed to create positive interactions with students throughout the school.

In such a proactive environment, careful personnel selection is important. Some school districts hire their own police officers; others employ city police services. Still other districts hire a combination of both district and municipal police, relying on the municipal members of the team to help coordinate prevention and enforcement activities. Costs for the community officers assigned to campuses often are shared between the police department and the school district.

Some schools hire their own security personnel instead of local police officers. These security personnel can support both immediate and long-range safety needs, but they vary greatly in the nature of their tasks. Some are armed, most are not. Some security officers are told to look specifically for such signs as bulging clothes or schoolbags, indicating that the student might be carrying a weapon. Their presence in hallways, stairwells, and other areas may act as deterrents to illicit behaviors.

Clearly, security officers should be screened for criminal records in the most rigorous way. Security officers who bully, control by overpowering, threaten, or otherwise show undesirable behaviors are both a short-term provocation and a long-term liability.

When fully trained, security officers should be able to describe all of the school's security services, from who controls keys and assigns badges to what words best describe the school's mission. They should be able to describe carefully how they carry out their duties, and why. However, security officers usually are paid very little for what can be a dangerous job, and positions frequently turn over. For these and many other reasons, trying to use security officer to provide wide-ranging support in a school can be challenging.

School officials also may work more informally with law enforcement personnel. Police can exchange information with school administrators on changes in gang dress, turf, signs, drugs, or weapon-related threats. Both police and juvenile justice workers should cooperate to reduce school truancy, because youth not in school and not employed are at increased risk for becoming either offenders or victims.

Balanced and Restorative Justice Programs

Some communities have adopted the "balanced and restorative justice" concept. That concept proposes three goals: protecting the community, insisting on criminals being accountable to victims for restitution, and developing competencies in offenders in order to prevent recidivism.

These programs place a strong focus on victims' rights. Victims can tell offenders about the impact of the crime on their lives, their families, their schools, and their communities. Victims have the right to observe the trial, unless they are to testify; they also have a right to know the offender's status, to be protected from intimidation and harassment, and to have access to counseling.

Balanced and restorative justice programs also are based on the belief that offenders need to know and understand the long-term consequences of their offenses. Mediation sessions between the victims and offenders, whether held in school or in juvenile facilities, are used to help offenders see the implications of their behavior, as well as to help the victims to heal emotionally (CCJJDP 1996).

Case Management Services

Social work case management can have a broad role in schools. Case managers can help at-risk students and families to navigate through the bureaucratic maze of available social services. Case workers can channel needy students into various forms of intervention, such as individual or small-group counseling, family therapy, rape prevention workshops, home counseling, or other appropriate services. Social workers often serve on student assistance teams.

Federal and State Safety Initiatives

The federal government supports a variety of local and state safety initiatives. For example, the 1993 Safe Schools Act supports grant-making initiatives, research, and technical assistance to support state and local programs. Federal agencies have cooperated with other organizations to study the problem of school violence. These agencies also gather information from various states on successful violence prevention and intervention efforts and disseminate what works to other states in written literature and electronically.

The U.S. Department of Justice Office of Juvenile Justice and Delinquency Prevention works with the U.S. Department of Education in the Safe and Drug-Free Schools Program to study ways to improve cooperation between juvenile justice and public school initiatives. Federal efforts produce materials on school safety and violence prevention and disseminate research on conflict resolution, parent involvement, school law programs, community policing, and related materials (see Resources).

State departments of education and health also have a vital role in violence prevention. State departments of education produce a variety of materials, from minimal "checklists of safety" to thoroughly researched documents on the causes of school violence, procedures for assessing school safety, and programs available in the state. Many state departments of education keep statewide databases on school violence incidents, help define data so that records are reported uniformly, and advocate strategies designed for special demographic areas and unique populations.

State departments of education often work closely with state departments of health since, in the last decade, it often has proved effective to conceptualize the problem of youth violence as a public health issue. State departments of health and education may jointly publish curricula to prevent school violence, develop pilot programs, and collect research on programs that are effective statewide (see Resources).

Finally, Project Head Start has a long and successful record of effective violence prevention among the very young. It is an early childhood intervention program that targets low-income children and their parents. Project Head Start develops children's intellectual skills, nurtures emotional and social growth, attends to children's mental and physical health needs, and builds community ties for parents with multiple needs. In the last decade, bipartisan nationwide research has demonstrated Project Head Start to be "among the most cost-effective inner-city crime and drug prevention strategies ever developed" (CDC 1993, p. 23).

Community-Based Organizations

Community-based organizations support cultures of nonviolence by providing youth activities during the critical hours after school lets out. Evidence accumulated over a number of years indicates that juveniles commit crimes most frequently after school: the incidence of juvenile crime tends to peak at 3:00 p.m. during the week (CCJJDP 1996). What happens after school is critical.

Community and business support services also play a critical role in helping keep school doors open after hours. Nonprofit organizations, community agencies, and dropout prevention programs such as Cities-in-Schools may bring mental health experts, counseling, and recreational opportunities to both parents and students after hours. These organizations also sponsor interesting student clubs, such as Olympics of the Mind, Double Dutch Jumping Jills, gospel chorus, chess, and many others. Library facilities, especially Internet access, would provide many parents with access to technology so they can familiarize themselves with important job skills. It also is an important consideration that a school that is open and inhabited by students and parents is less vulnerable to vandalism than is an empty, dark, locked school.

Unfortunately, funding after-school or weekend activities can be very difficult. Many programs are required to show results in one or two fiscal years, the length of a funding "pilot." But it can take much more time to improve the lives of at-risk youth. Many programs cannot demonstrate concrete results in so short a time; and when they are de-funded, it often hurts those youth who have begun to rely on these programs.

When considering community resources, it is important to remember volunteers. Volunteers play an important role in the schools. Many serve as mentors, changing the lives of youth one boy or girl at a time. Others read to at-risk children or perform a variety of other tasks for the school. They often are positive role models for students.

Local churches also offer important support services for schools. It does not matter if a local church is Native American, Moslem, Hindu, Christian, Jewish, or any other faith; almost all local churches will have positive effects on youth. Churches provide moral imperatives for youths. During high-risk, after-school hours, churches also provide activities that not only occupy youths' time but also fill that time with camaraderie-building, conscience-raising, thoughtful activities.

Community and school sports activities have traditionally attracted large numbers of students at risk for school violence. After school is a great time for sports activities, but the complicated world of sports and sports' hero worship has been both a blessing and a curse to school leaders wishing to nurture a peaceful culture. Opposing arguments have been made regarding whether sports participation deters or encourages aggression and crime.

The key to organized sports is to keep the priorities straight. Students must learn that safety and nonviolent behavior are higher priorities than winning, regardless of the emotions involved in many games. Sports activities should be viewed as only a part of the total youth-building program. In proper perspective, sports give students appropriate role models, opportunities to socialize with peers, and recognition when hard work pays off in a victory. These benefits do emerge from well-organized and expertly coached sports programs. The National School Safety Center recommends that all organizations involved in sports should consider the following preventive measures:

- Establish clear behavior expectations and rules.
- Have students, coaches, athletes, and staff discuss their roles and proper behavior.
- Implement antiviolence lessons or curricula.
- Train supervisors to intervene when needed.
- Establish peer mediation and conflict resolution programs so that youth will know how to de-escalate an incident before it explodes (NSSC 1992, p. 3).

Specific concrete prevention strategies should be considered before any major sports events. School officials should:

- Talk with the coaches, booster clubs, game officials, students, and police to determine their concerns and to ask for support.
- Identify local resources to help supervise the crowds and to respond to emergencies.

- Develop a communication plan and an effective communication network.
- Designate a command post.
- Specify who is in charge.
- Graffiti, after being read and recorded, should be thoroughly removed.
- Parking lots should be well-lit and supervised.
- Ensure that entrances and exits, concessions, and bathrooms for visiting and home teams are separated (NSSC 1992, p. 2).

Members of both schools' crisis response teams should be present at sporting events and should be in communication with local law authorities, providing back-up when needed. Visible signs of authority are particularly helpful at sporting events. Teachers and administrators, of course, should be present and aware of safety concerns. Uniformed police officers, security guards, and bike and foot patrols also make a highly visible statement about expectations for behavior. Some schools have requested police helicopters to fly over the games as an added symbol of the police presence (NSSC 1992).

Finally, schools should cooperate with the local neighborhood watch program. When the school and community act together, they can ensure the neighborhood watch program is active and functioning well. Neighborhood watch groups report crimes and suspicious activities; they also can be trained to observe harassment among students or other specific dangers in the area. School personnel, including crossing guards, should work with the neighborhood watch group to report suspicious activities.

Professional and Private Organizations

Almost every education organization has published books, articles, videos, guidelines, and statements on the topic of school violence. The National School Safety Council (NSSC) has provided educators with background materials and technical assistance on the subject of school violence for many years. Most professional libraries in schools have, or should have, a variety of materials on school safety published by professional organizations. Educators are wise to read widely and currently from these professional materials (see Resources).

The Media

The mass media are part of the problem, but they also can be part of the solution. Schools must learn to make the media part of the team that can make schools safe. However, there are several guidelines that school administrators should follow when dealing with the media.

First, while school administrators should try to set the tone of any conversations with reporters, they also should be honest. It is unwise to try to deny the number of crime incidents in a school. However, if officials have adequate handouts, articles, and supporting materials on school safety plans ready for reporters, the reports can be channeled away from alarmist headlines and toward an attitude of providing information in order to gather support.

Second, school leaders should regularly advertise their school safety plan in the local media and in brochures. Districts and schools with websites also should include the plan there.

Third, one member of the crisis management team (see Chapter Four) should be specially trained to work with the reporters who will converge at the school following an incident. That individual should have training in how to maintain control of the interview, how to clarify ground rules and objectives, how to predict public reactions to media reports, and how to prevent panic. Even the smallest school district news interview can be picked up by the national news services, so crisis media liaisons are proactive about contacting the media, are trained and prepared for the interview, and focus on responses that will meet the victims' needs.

By maintaining honest, engaging, and responsible communications with the press in daily events as well as in crises, schools form powerful ties with the media. Thus the news media will be more likely to report successful school-based interventions. Few news media will call a school on their own to solicit information about what is working, so making the media a source of support begins with school officials.

References

Bazemore, G., and Day, S. "Restoring the Balance: Juvenile and Community Justice." *Juvenile Justice* 3 (December 1996): 3-14.

Centers for Disease Control (CDC). *The Prevention of Youth Violence.* Washington, D.C.: U.S. Department of Health and Human Services, 1993.

Coordinating Council on Juvenile Justice and Delinquency Prevention (CCJJDP). *Combating Violence and Delinquency: The National Juvenile Justice Action Plan.* Washington D.C., March 1996.

Hechinger, Fred. *Fateful Choices: Executive Summary.* New York: Carnegie Council on Adolescent Development, April 1992.

Lane, Kenneth E.; Richardson, Michael D.; and VanBerkum, Dennis W., eds. *The School Safety Handbook: Taking Action for Student and Staff Protection.* Lancaster, Pa.: Technomic, 1996.

National School Safety Center (NSSC). "Working on a Game Plan for Safety." *School Safety Update* (September 1992).

Office of Juvenile Justice and Delinquency Prevention (OJJDP). "Gang Suppression and Intervention." *OJJDP Summary* (October 1994): 3.

Remb= Remb. Rembold, Carole. *Solving Violence Problems in Your School.* Minneapolis: Johnson Institute, 1994.

Williams, Sheriff R.M., "On Patrol with Deputy Perkins, School Liaison Officer." *Sheriff Times* 1 (Summer 1996): 2.

Chapter Seven

Building a Nonviolent Culture

Despite numerous arguments about public schools, they have remained the primary institution in which conversations occur about the welfare of America's children. The skills of conflict resolution and anger management are at the very heart of what it means to be educated in a democracy. Our children's welfare depends on our schools teaching them how to stay safe and get along.

Nurturing these characteristics is no longer an option. The population of youth served by schools has changed over the years, and schools must meet evolving needs. Schools must lead the way in a powerful coalition for preventing violence. As John Goodlad notes: "Just as education serves to close the gap between society's needs and society's goals, it also serves to push out the horizons of what could be. It is civilization's most significant process for determining what a society might become" (Goodlad 1994, p. 16).

Schools do not need to have every resource or program in place to help children. But they do need several important things: teachers who care deeply, mentors, interesting programs and activities. When a school neglects these things, it has failed its most basic moral responsibilities.

It is impossible for a school to start too early. Representatives from the parents' organization should visit each new parent in the community and help celebrate the beginning of three or four years of preschool learning by leaving a few materials or information about parenting classes. Schools should make special efforts to help teenage mothers.

Student involvement is critical. The same peer pressure that pushes students to be cool, bully others, and fight can be applied to new goals — to resolve conflicts and accept differences.

Educators and parents do not need further research. The statistics are clear and compelling. Spiraling rates of child poverty, saturation of neighborhoods by guns, the attractions of drugs, and poor parenting have led to a loss of hope — a pervasive nihilism among the nation's most vulnerable youth. This crisis can and must be addressed by the one institution currently able to reach the most children: schools.

Safe schools reach out to parents. They teach parents to solve their own problems nonviolently so that they provide good role models for their children. And they teach parents how to help their kids work things out with words, clearly defining where child discipline ends and abuse begins. Safe schools arrange home visits by teachers and volunteers to reach those parents who do not attend school activities, and they involve churches, businesses, and other community groups to reach these families. They even may assign volunteers to meet parents in the parking lot as they drop their children off in the morning.

The vision of the school as an exporter of peace requires school leaders to hire relationship-centered staff. There is no doubt that the school's role is changing; it now must assess children's needs more holistically in order to meet both their academic and social concerns. Changing visions of school require that principals select teachers whose repertoires include a wide variety of human relations skills. Teachers must be willing to cooperate and initiate contact with social workers, police, psychologists, parole officers, and clergy to extend the reach of the classroom community into the child's home. Principals must find the best ways to match the available services to the children's diverse needs.

Where does a school's responsibility end? As schools attempt to meet the increasing needs of students and to determine how to keep students safe, new definitions of "school" will emerge and new boundaries will be drawn.

Just gathering resources and programs is not enough. Rather, most important is the belief of everyone in the school that violence is intolerable and no one has to accept it, that life is precious and to be respected, and that communities should be characterized by conflict resolution and cooperation.

The time has passed for educators to pretend they can coerce students, dominate them, or humiliate them into anything. Children saturated by environmental violence do not coerce easily. They resist domination and are seldom humiliated by adults. Attempting to eliminate or reduce school violence by force is like throwing gasoline on a match; it only makes matters worse.

Instead, safety begins by modeling a different way of thinking and believing that builds respect and caring among those for whom respect is a rare commodity. Violent children may appear calloused, and many are; but their behavior covers fragile egos in a frightening world. Confident, caring educators who believe in nonviolence will be the key to saving these children. Only they can create a peaceable school.

References

Goodlad, John I. *What Schools Are For*. 2nd ed. Bloomington, Ind.: Phi Delta Kappa Educational Foundation, 1994.

Selected Resources

Extensive resources are now available to schools interested in violence prevention. The following resources are listed because they reflect the underlying values of this book: 1) that prevention programs must be comprehensive and systemic; 2) that good programs are based on clearly stated beliefs about all children, and 3) that good violence prevention does not have to be expensive. There are undoubtedly many excellent programs not on this list. This should be considered as a starter list of successful resources that are time-tested, well-researched, and carefully evaluated.

Center to Prevent Handgun Violence
1225 Eye Street, N.W.
Suite 1100
Washington, DC 20005
(202) 289-7319
Fax: (202) 408-1851
http://www.hci-ctphv.org

The Center to Prevent Handgun Violence runs public awareness campaigns to improve people's knowledge, attitudes, and behaviors concerning the protection they believe firearms offer. This nonpartisan, nonprofit foundation also offers information and programs on the safe storage of firearms, instructing children about handgun safety, checking firearms before cleaning, and respecting the power of firearms to hurt and kill. The center has produced "Straight Talk About Risks" (STAR), which alerts school-age youth to the dangers of handguns. This program also helps youths develop victim prevention skills and learn to manage such problems as conflict or peer pressure nonviolently and without guns. STAR's curriculum, with its primary focus on problem-solving skills and life-saving behaviors, reflects state-of-the-art research and evaluation.

Education Development Center, Inc.
55 Chapel Street
Newton, MA 02160
(617) 969-7100
Fax: (412) 741-0609

The Education Development Center produces the "Violence Prevention Curriculum for Adolescents" by Deborah Prothrow-Stith. This program teaches that anger is a normal part of life and can be channeled into productive activities and habits. One of the pioneers of the movement to see violence as a public health issue, Prothrow-Stith employs role-playing, observation, and class discussions about "fight/flight," media violence, consequences to behavior, and other topics to increase students' ability to prevent injury to themselves and violence to others.

Educators for Social Responsibility
23 Garden Street
Cambridge, MA 02138
(617) 492-1764
www.esrnational.org

ESR offers programs in conflict resolution for youth from early childhood to high school. Services include staff development workshops, mixed-media instructional resources, teacher leadership workshops, demonstrations, discussion facilitation, and specific skills development for teachers in such areas as conflict resolution, violence prevention, prejudice reduction, emotional expression, and multicultural awareness.

Farmers Insurance Group of Companies
PO Box 4989
Los Angeles, CA 90051-9723
1-800-204-7722 or (213) 964-8039
E-mail: taphrp@aol.com

Farmers Insurance distributes *The American Promise*, which includes videotapes for grades 1-5 and 6-9 and a loose-leaf binder of coordinated lessons. The program focuses on maintaining peace and freedom through involvement. Themes include the effects of corruption, volunteering, media critiquing, community-building, communication, and finding common ground. Last updated in 1996, the program includes a bibliography. The kit is free on request.

Illinois Institute for Dispute Resolution
National Peaceable School Project
110 West Main Street
Urbana, IL. 61801
(217) 384-4118
Fax: (217) 384-8280

The Illinois Institute for Dispute Resolution (IIDR) suggests peer mediation training in six developmental phases: 1) develop the program team and commitment, 2) design and plan the program, 3) select and train the mediators, 4) educate a critical mass, 5) develop and execute a promotional campaign, and 6) program operation and maintenance. Technical assistance and follow-up are provided.

Interaction Book Company
7208 Cornelia Drive
Edina, MN 55435
(612) 831-9500
Fax: (414) 783-5906

Interaction Book Company publishes the curriculum resources and other materials by David W. and Roger T. Johnson, developers of cooperative learning techniques. *Teaching Students to Be Peacemakers* (1991) and *Reducing School Violence Through Conflict Resolution* (1996) discuss constructive conflict, negotiation, anger management, and conflict mediation as a natural extension of cooperative learning in the classroom. Technical assistance is also available through the Cooperative Learning and Conflict Resolution Center in Minneapolis, which can be reached at (612) 624-7031 or http://134/84/183/54/.

Johnson Institute
7205 Ohms Lane
Minneapolis, MN 55439-2159
1-800-231-5156
Fax: (612) 831-1631
http://www.johnsoninstitute.com
E-mail: info@johnsoninstitute.com

The Johnson Institute offers a wide variety of materials in diverse media for teachers, administrators, parents, and youth workers focusing on violence prevention and alcoholism. Of particular interest is a strong series about "entitlement" (how environments and individuals may unconsciously allow violence to continue). Many materials are designed to increase parental awareness and support for prevention. The institute publishes *Respect & Protect: A Practical, Step-by-Step Violence Prevention and Intervention Program for Schools and Communities* by Carole Remboldt and Richard Zimman, which includes a guide, video, and books that emphasize systemic program development. Also of interest is the National Intervention Network, which provides a referral network of individuals trained in the Johnson Institute intervention model.

National Center for Injury Prevention and Control
Centers for Disease Control and Prevention
4770 Buford Highway NE
Mail Stop F36
Atlanta, Georgia 30341
1-888-232-3228 or (404) 488-4646

The Centers for Disease Control (CDC) created a framework for community action, "The Prevention of Youth Violence," which provides a logical format for school and community initiatives. Well-researched and practical, the guide suggests prevention strategies and tools to evaluate individual school and community progress and lists a number of other agencies and how to contact them.

National Crime Prevention Council
1700 K Street, N.W., Second Floor
Washington, D.C. 20006-3817
(202) 466-6272
Fax: (202) 296-1356
http://www.weprevent.org

The National Crime Prevention Council assists individual cities to place crime prevention high on their agendas. The organization's numerous initiatives include national campaign organization, leadership development, short- and long-term initiative development, and interagency cooperation. Information about the neighborhood watch and crime watch programs is available at http://www.masterlock.com/crimer.html.

National Crisis Prevention Institute, Inc.
3315-K North 124th Street
Brookfield, WI 53005
1-800-558-8976
(414) 783-5906
E-mail: cpi@execpc.com

CPI training programs, instructional materials, and videos focus on intervention in situations of imminent danger. CPI would be appropriate in situations where teachers and students need specific and immediate help in managing violent confrontations, physical assaults, disruptive students, weapons possession, and other aggressive behaviors. While not the most helpful materials available to define the school's safety mission or guide program choice, CPI provides strategies to reduce danger in environments where violence has been tolerated and fear needs to be greatly reduced.

National Educational Service
1252 North Loesch Road
P.O. Box 8
Bloomington, IN 47402
1-888-763-9045 or (812) 336-7700
Fax: (812) 336-7790
http://www.nes.org
E-mail: nes@nes.org

National Educational Service uses a variety of media to deal with such areas as breaking the cycle of violence, anger management, bullying, and overcoming despair. The award-winning video, "Reclaiming Youth at Risk: Our Hope for the Future," uses the four Sioux concepts of belonging, mastery, independence, and generosity in a program found to significantly reduce incidents of violence among high-risk students. NES also publishes *Reaching Today's Youth: The Community Circle of Caring Journal* and a variety of other resources.

National School Boards Association
1680 Duke Street
Alexandria, VA 22314
(703) 838-6722
Fax: (703) 683-7590

The National School Board Association (NSBA) fosters the education of school board members about 1) overcoming denial about school violence, 2) sharing information about programs that work, 3) advocating comprehensive change, and 4) linking appropriate agencies into networks that support school safety. *Violence in the Schools: How America's Schoolboards Are Safeguarding Your Children* (1993), part of the NSBA Best Practices Series, contains suggestions to increase violence prevention efforts, parent involvement, student and faculty confidence in the school's safety, and policies to promote peace. Names and phone numbers for school districts and contact individuals are available in categories related to such topics as "home-school linkages," "conflict resolution/mediation training/peer mediation," and "work opportunities."

National School Safety Center
4165 Thousand Oaks Blvd.
Suite 290
West Lake Village, CA 91362
(805) 373-9977
Fax: (805) 373-9277
http://www.NSSC1.org

The mission of the NSSC is to preserve and extend school violence prevention efforts. This nonprofit organization offers technical assistance to schools, including site visits, publications on school safety issues, and legal assistance. NSSC Resource Papers offer current research on such topics as gang suppression, sports and school violence, and school safety design.

Peaceful Resistance
D&R Games
P.O. Box 199044
Indianapolis, IN 46219
(317) 899-8326
http://www.indy.net/~gnldad/peacresi.html
E-mail: gnldad@indy.net (Dave Thornburg)

Peaceful Resistance is a board game inspired by Gandhi and recognized in *Games Magazine*'s buyer's guide issue. The creator of the game explains that it is based on Gandhi's 240-mile march to the sea to make salt. The game encourages players to come up with peaceful ways in order to win.

Resolving Conflict Creatively Program
163 3rd Ave., #103
New York, NY 10003
(212) 387-0225
Fax: (212) 387-0510
http://www.benjerry.com/esr/

The Resolving Conflict Creatively Program (RCCP) is a comprehensive, K-12 school-based program in conflict resolution and intergroup relations that provides a model for preventing violence and creating caring learning communities. It began in 1985 as a collaboration between Educators for Social Responsibility Metropolitan Area (ESR Metro) and the New York City Board of Education. It is now the largest program of its kind in the country. It is distributed nationally by the Educators for Social Responsibility.

RCCP provides teachers with in-depth training, curricula, and extensive staff development support; establishes student peer mediation programs; offers parent workshops; and conducts leadership training for school administrators. Districts make a three- to five-year commitment.

ESR also offers many other programs to schools and districts with more limited resources.

Second Step Program
Committee for Children
2203 Airport Way South, Suite 500
Seattle, WA 98134-2027
(206) 343-1223
Fax: (206) 343-1445

Second Step is a violence prevention curriculum for grades PreK-K; 1-3, 4-5, and 6-8. The program focuses on reducing impulsive and aggressive behaviors by building empathy, controlling impulses, solving problems peacefully, and managing anger. Role-playing, teacher modeling of desired behaviors, and stories with discussion form the basis of the curriculum.

SouthEastern Regional Vision for Education
Florida Department of Education Prevention Center
345 S. Magnolia Drive, Suite D-23
Tallahassee, FL 32301-2950
1-800-352-6001 or (904) 922-2300
Fax: (904) 922-2286
http://www.serve.org

The Florida Department of Education Prevention Center was an early leader in state initiatives to prevent school violence. It assists schools and districts in developing comprehensive programs for a diverse population. Of particular interest is *Hot Topics: Usable Research on Reducing School Violence in Florida* (1993) by Kadel and Follman, which looks at the state's response to causes and consequences of student violence, crisis management, strategies to prevent violence, and resources.

Teaching Tolerance
Southern Poverty Law Center
400 Washington Ave.
Montgomery, AL 36104
Fax: (334) 264-3121

The Shadow of Hate is one of the four excellent video-based teaching aids available to prevent race-based violence in the classroom. Based on the idea that democracy is still a "work in progress," Teaching Tolerance materials examine America's history of prejudice with an eye toward greater appreciation of and responsibility for maintaining freedom in our nation. An excellent teaching guide centers on themes as well as on concrete historical understanding. The initial set is free to principals; subsequent sets and materials are priced very reasonably.

U.S. Department of Education
600 Maryland Ave., S.W.
Washington, DC 20202
1-800-424-1616
Fax: (202) 219-1817
http://www.ed.gov
E-mail: acceric@inet.ed.gov
Safe and Drug-Free Schools (a division of OERI)
Phone: 1-800-624-0100 or (202) 260-3954

The Safe and Drug-Free Schools Program and the U.S. Department of Education recently published *Connections*, which analyzes the relative long-term merits of various drug, alcohol, and violence prevention programs. *Connections* is a free kit that includes two videotapes and an audiotape, two posters, and other teacher aids. It focuses on building resilience in the children of high-risk parents, particularly alcoholics. The kit includes specific ways to build resilience and empathy in those clearly at risk for becoming alcoholics themselves and for suffering child abuse and neglect. Particular attention is paid to children of Native Americans and other high-risk groups.

U.S. Department of Justice
Office of Juvenile Justice & Delinquency Prevention
Juvenile Justice Clearinghouse
P.O. Box 6000
Rockville, MD 20849-6000
1-800- 638-8736
Fax: (800) 638-8736
http://www.ncjrs.org/ojjhome.htms
E-mail: askncjrs@ncjrs.org

The Office of Juvenile Justice & Delinquency Prevention and the Safe and Drug-Free Schools Program of the U.S. Department of Education co-publish *Conflict Resolution Education: A Guide to Implementing Programs in Schools, Youth-Serving Organizations, and Community and Juvenile Justice Settings*, which is edited by Donna Crawford and Richard Bodine. This excellent implementation guide includes several approaches to preventing school violence. The Office of Juvenile Justice & Delinquency Prevention also has extensive materials available free to help K-12 educators bridge the gap between the juvenile justice system and schools.

The department also disseminates *Rising Above Gangs and Drugs: How to Start a Community Reclamation Project*, based on the work of the Community Reclamation Project in Lomita, California. This book is a very practical guide with suggestions for community assessment, budgeting, staff selection, office procedures, building community identity, creating newsletters, publicity, corporate sponsorship, and other topics.

Violence in Schools: Solutions that Work
The Learning Channel
http://school.discovery.com/vvault/ttv/spring96/wk06.html
E-mail: school@discovery.com

Teacher TV: Violence in the Schools — Solutions that Work is a video on violence intervention, students controlling the playground, kids' court, and class consciousness. One response to the increasing violence in schools has been to install metal detectors and conduct weapons searches. But has this stopped the violence? Kids respond.

About the Author

Vicky Schreiber Dill is a senior researcher for the National Center for Alternative Teacher Certification Information at the Haberman Educational Foundation. The NCATCI is a nonprofit organization dedicated to working with poor, at-risk children. Dill also trains principals to select the best teachers for working in high-poverty schools, including teachers who will help reduce violence in the schools.

Dill is the author of *Closing the Gap: Acceleration Versus Remediation and the Impact of Retention in Grade on Student Achievement* (Texas Education Agency, 1993) and *Alternative Teacher Certification: History, Handbook, and How To* (Haberman Foundation, 1996). She also is the author or co-author of book chapters and articles on school violence, teacher selection and alternative teacher certification, retention in grade, multiage education, and the role of emotions in school.

Dill taught high school English and middle school developmental reading for nine years. She also taught gifted education at the Texas Governor's School for the Gifted in 1989 and 1990 and was an assistant professor of education and director of student teaching and early field experiences at St. Cloud State University.

Dill received her master's in curriculum and social foundations of education from the University of Pennsylvania. Her Ph.D. in early American literature is from the University of Notre Dame.

Dill is the mother of three children and currently lives in McPherson, Kansas.